'This is an excellent guide – thorough, practical and challenging. Working in the field of African Diasporean studies, I have found it rare to come across a book that addresses Equal Opportunities issues in such a direct and helpful manner. A must.'

(Brendan Simon, tutor in Caribbean Studies)

'I find that English Studies texts are often more complicated than they need to be – not to mention dry and boring. *How to Write* is different because it is "user-friendly". . . It is one of the most constructive books I've ever read.'

(Carol Cook, Postgraduate Diploma in English Studies student)

'As a mature student returning to A level study twenty-five years after writing my last school essay, I found the book invaluable. I liked the practical, nuts-and-bolts approach, and the fact that suggestions are applicable to all levels of study. I am sure this will be a useful handbook for people in my position for many years to come.'

(Larry Stabbins, professional musician)

'A well-designed and practical handbook, with plenty of examples and exercises, which are genuinely useful because sufficiently precise . . . As a student, I found it clear, easy-to-read and enjoyable; and as a teacher I intend to use it with my own students.'

(Dr Helen Reid-Thomas, postgraduate Masters student and tutor at the Institute for Applied Language Studies, Edinburgh University)

How to Write Essays, Dissertations and Theses in Literary Studies

Nigel Fabb and *Alan Durant*

Longman
London and New York

Longman Group Limited
Longman House, Burnt Mill,
Harlow, Essex CM20 2JE, England
and Associated Companies throughout the world.

Published in the United States of America
by Longman Publishing, New York

© Longman Group UK Limited 1993

First published 1993
Third impression 1995

ISBN 0 582 08977 8

British Library Cataloguing-in-Publication Data

A catalogue record for this book is
available from the British Library

Library of Congress Cataloging-in-Publication Data

Fabb, Nigel, 1958–
How to write essays, dissertations, and theses in literary studies/
Nigel Fabb and Alan Durant.
    p. cm.
Includes bibliographical references and index.
ISBN 0-582-08977-8 (ppr)
1. Criticism – Authorship. 2. Literature – History and criticism – Theory,
etc. 3. Dissertations, Academic – Authorship. 4. English language – Rhetoric.
5. Essay – Authorship. I. Durant, Alan. II. Title
PE1479.C7F33 1993
808'. 0668–dc20   92-46686
                                                              CIP

Set by 7 in 10/12 pt Bembo
Produced through Longman Malaysia, GPS

Contents

Contents

List of exercises

Preface

You may have come to this book because you are studying for an examination – 'A' or 'S' level, GCSE or Scottish Higher. Or you may be starting a course in Higher or Further Education, as an undergraduate or postgraduate. Perhaps you have found essays easy in the past but need to adapt to new and different writing demands; perhaps you are about to write your first extended essay, dissertation or thesis. Or perhaps you have never written an essay in literary studies before – a situation true even for some postgraduates. Whatever stage you are at now, you are likely to benefit from a review of the problems to be faced in writing essays, and from learning a range of strategies for tackling – with skill and confidence – exam questions, essay topics and higher level research.

In your classes or your research you will need to perform a range of different sorts of writing tasks. Each presents its own challenges. Exams require specialised skills in managing your writing in the time allowed, just as much as they require your knowledge. Coursework essays, projects and dissertations require still more complex skills in preparing, organising and presenting your material. The necessary arguments are likely to be more complex than those you must organise in a short exam answer; and the demands for detailed illustration and explanation will be greater. So a systematic approach to your planning and writing is indispensable.

Many students faced with a writing assignment feel almost defeated from the outset, downcast by the idea that there are just good writers and bad writers. And undoubtedly the quality of essays is affected by the personal aptitude and enthusiasm an individual brings to the task. But the process of writing academic essays also involves a distinct set of skills, conventions and methods which can be learned and practised. There are also established strategies for avoiding many of the pitfalls. By spending some time exploring the rules and methods of essay-writing, therefore, and by monitoring closely your own work-in-progress, you should be able to improve your effectiveness in presenting your ideas and arguments, and so improve your chances of achievement and success in your coursework and exams.

In writing this book we have tried to produce a guide to essay-writing which takes into account two large-scale changes in English studies over the last twenty years. Firstly, there has been a shift away from assessment just on the basis of short answers written in the exam hall; instead, a variety of longer coursework essays, portfolios and projects is often now required, and these demand specialised techniques and skills. Secondly, with the fundamental redefinition of literary studies brought about by the increased influence of literary and cultural theory, new styles and demands of argumentation have emerged, which any guide to writing essays needs to recognise and respond to. We should emphasise, nevertheless, that the usefulness of this book is not confined to students of English studies. Although our examples are taken from courses and student research in English Literature, most of what we say is applicable to writing essays on literature in other languages, such as French, German, Spanish or Latin, as well as to courses in cultural studies, media studies, art history and other fields. The conventions and strategies we discuss apply in all courses where essays of literary or cultural analysis are written in English.

In the chapters which follow, we work through the process of writing an essay, dissertation or thesis step by step, offering at each stage concrete guidelines and detailed commentary on examples selected from student work. At the same time, we reflect on the assumptions and difficulties of the various methods and techniques we introduce. This is to enable you to take advantage of the norms or conventional devices of essay-writing without necessarily being prevented from further development of your individual writing talents by fixed dos and donts. In this way, we hope that *How to Write Essays, Dissertations and Theses in Literary Studies* will serve as a manual that you can consult at each stage of working on a project in hand – for ideas, general guidelines and specific practical suggestions.

Acknowledgements

We are grateful to the following for their help with the preparation of this book: Raja Naseem Akhtar, Eman Abd El Ati, Mairi John Blackings, Margaret Fabb, Leena Ibrahim, Rania Kassem, Paulina Kewes, Woohak Lee, Stuart Lucas, Stuart McCaw, Christina Martin, Alice Robotham, Rebecca Thomas.

Introduction

THE IMPORTANCE OF WRITING

A lot of the interest in studying literature comes from reading books, and so does a lot of the pleasure. A literature course can seem mainly a process of reading through (and learning about) a series of prescribed works; in doing so, you develop the required sense of the literary and historical subject matter, and so become proficient in the discipline.

It is true that 'input' in literary studies is largely made up of what you **read** and how you read it. But the assessed 'output' consists of **writing** – whether this takes the form of short written answers to prescribed questions (as in examinations) or of extended coursework essays, dissertations and theses. This (and not your work in class or seminar discussion) is usually all that is directly assessed; and it is this situation which leads some people to believe that it is possible to succeed in literary studies *primarily* on the basis of specialised essay-writing skills and formulas. Although such a claim is essentially misguided, it nevertheless captures an important point: that careful and sensitive reading counts for little in a course in literary studies unless it is linked to specialised skills in constructing arguments on the written page. **Your success in reading is invisible to others unless you also know how to write**.

This book is about the writing and study skills which support essay-writing. It investigates how you embody the observations you make about literary texts in appropriate written forms. We work step by step through the processes involved in writing: interpreting a prescribed question, or thinking of a title or topic of your own; working out your basic ideas; making a first sketch or outline; using reference sources to fill out your ideas with appropriate information; developing your argument coherently, from its introduction through to its conclusion; monitoring aspects of composition such as grammar, spelling and cohesion; and submitting your finished work in a recognised academic format.

By investigating and making suggestions about each of these topics, this book should help you break down the sometimes confusing overall experience of writing an essay into a series of distinguishable stages, each of which you can analyse and learn to control.

FOUR BASIC PRINCIPLES

We begin with four basic claims about writing:

(a) Writing means construction.
(b) Writing involves a constant process of reconstruction.
(c) Writing is a way of thinking.
(d) Writing is different from talking.

After discussing each of these basic claims, we raise some practical questions about how you can use this book to develop and improve your study and writing skills.

(a) Writing means construction

Throughout this book we treat writing less as an activity of immediate self-expression, in which you pour out ideas spontaneously and inspirationally, and more as a process of composition, in the sense of making or building.

It is often said that books are read many times but are written only once. In the case of essays written for literature courses, it may be more helpful to think of them as generally having to be *written* (in the sense of modified, altered or drafted) many times, and then probably read by your reader only once.

Accordingly, you need to learn how to steer the repeated stages of writing and rewriting which enable first thoughts to be directed into a sustained argument. Many of the difficulties which arise in writing an essay are created by the need to control a number of different aspects of organisation at the same time. You need to control:

– the argument, at a conceptual level;
– the essay's information structure, to avoid presenting, as if they

2

were new, facts or views likely to be well-known to and presupposed by your reader;
- the discourse structure, so that your essay builds up, and has shape and development;
- the style, so that the essay speaks with a voice you are comfortable with (and so that it does not become too repetitive, pompous or colloquial);
- the punctuation and grammar, so that the essay can be read easily and unambiguously;
- the presentation, so that the essay can be read clearly, in terms of layout, handwriting and typeface.

(b) Writing involves a constant process of reconstruction

Everyone has heard of writers who gestate an idea mentally for a long period and then write it down, perfectly formed. But such writers are in a minority, and most writing – whether it takes the form of poetry, committee reports, memos and minutes of meetings, or literary essays – passes through successive revisions and is modified in the light of what a given expression of ideas actually looks like on the page. You can best reflect on your writing once it is on the page, rather than trying to shape it while it is just an idea in your head. Writing down sketches, headings, and trial sequences of ideas is good practice. This approach challenges the common belief (which you may still hear from traditional teachers and research supervisors) that you should start by doing all your reading, and only then begin writing. For the recommendation that you should do all your reading first, in order to have something to write when you start, is in our view misguided. Writing helps you understand what it is that you need from the books you are reading, and points you towards other books – and particular facts and arguments in them – that you will need to read but haven't yet thought of. For this reason, abstract intentions and theoretical knowledge of good writing must take a back seat to the practical approach of 'try it on the page and see what it looks like'.

(c) Writing is a way of thinking

Your writing is a product of your thinking, a product which you exchange in a course for a grade or marks. But it is not just a *product* of your thinking – it *is* your thinking. Writing is a tool – like diagrams, maps or numerical calculations – for thinking with and for organising ideas in sequences and systems that cannot easily be held simultaneously in the mind. It is also a tool that you carry with you into domains beyond

3

literary studies: a so-called 'transferable skill'. One of the historical arguments for literary studies as a worthwhile discipline is that it provides training in thinking; this book shows you how to make the writing process central to this training.

It can be important to hold to the idea of writing as a tool for thinking with, especially when you doubt the worth of what you are writing because it has no real addressee. (Teachers or examiners, after all, are supposed to be precisely those people *who already know what you are going to tell them.*) Irrespective of who reads your essays, they provide opportunities for you to develop solutions to the intellectual problems that you identify or set yourself; they offer ways of thinking through questions in a more reflective and considered form than is likely to be possible in most spoken contexts of conversation or discussion. In this way, writing an essay may provide a degree of satisfaction – and increased self-confidence – at least as valuable as the marks with which it is rewarded.

(d) Writing is different from talking

When you talk to someone your hearer can tell you whether or not she understands what you are saying by her expression, gestures, or by explicitly telling you so. She can stop you and ask you to explain or clarify something. But your *reader* cannot stop you to ask for clarification, and you cannot ask your reader whether she has understood. So you need to provide everything essential for understanding when you compose the written text; you can't rephrase any parts which didn't get across the first time. This is one reason why writing is typically more formal and bound by more explicit rules than speaking is.

But 'providing everything essential' creates problems of its own. If you provide too much background information your reader will become bored and lose attention. So you need constantly to make decisions, as precisely as possible, about how much information your reader will need by way of background and how much can simply be assumed.

The direction or development of what you write is important, too. Your writing must appear to lead towards a particular goal which is signalled clearly, rather than merely listing or presenting material the relevance of which has not been explicitly established. In this respect there is a useful check you can make on yourself: imagine yourself as a reader of your work who is constantly asking: *why is she/he telling me this?*

PRACTICE

Because writing is different from speech it is possible to think of writing as a 'foreign language': most people use written English with less fluency than they use spoken English. And improving your writing is rather like improving your use of a foreign language: practice helps. Practice in essay-writing involves first putting boundaries around a writing task. For example, you can set a time limit of forty minutes, and try to write a complete essay in this time (using old examination questions, perhaps); learning how to do this means learning how to plan and time your work, and is of course useful in examinations. You should judge your success *given the time permitted*. Alternatively, practice can mean taking special care over one small piece of work. You can take a fairly self-contained page or short section or paragraph from an essay and keep rewriting it, analysing the results of successive revisions. Try carrying out different parts of a task, in isolation from the overall process of writing an essay. Work out what a question is asking you, without trying to answer it; make a list of paragraph headings for large numbers of essays that you never intend actually to write in full. Learn from your practice (and take notes of what you have learned) so that the next time you can avoid repeating mistakes by adopting general writing strategies that you have already used successfully on a previous occasion.

WILL THIS BOOK SOLVE ALL YOUR WRITING PROBLEMS FOR YOU?

This book makes suggestions about how to write essays, dissertations and theses in literary studies, suggestions which range from how to think up a topic, through how to create an appropriate written tone, to how to avoid spelling mistakes. None of these suggestions are rules. Rules for writing can inhibit originality, stifle your imaginative involvement in literature, cramp your style and turn literary study into a production line of variations on the same basic model. We intend to **enable** (not to prescribe) by offering ideas, models and suggestions for you to use if they seem preferable to what you have done in the past or are faced with doing now. Throughout, we emphasise that you should *adapt* (or simply understand and then disagree with) our suggestions, creatively and for your own purposes. There is no single correct way to write an essay, and it would be impossible to predict all the possible ways in which a good essay could be put together.

Literary studies as a discipline is strongly committed to subjectivity and individuality, partly for reasons associated with the history of the discipline and partly because of the complexity, subjectivity and individuality of literature itself. (We discuss literary studies in more detail in two other textbooks which supplement this one: Durant and Fabb, *Literary Studies in Action*, and Montgomery et al. *Ways of Reading: Advanced Reading Skills for Students of Literature*.) Individuality and originality are even valued by some teachers to the extent that an off-beat and slightly idiosyncratic essay may be rewarded more than one which is clear and competent but lacks any distinctive flair. Remember, though, that even the most individual work exists in a context of established conventions about the sorts of topic which are studied, how to investigate them, how to write about them, what kind of language to use, how to structure and present an essay, and so on. You need to know what the established conventions are, so that you can work with (or against) them, without being limited or dominated by them.

This book presents the conventions. It can be seen as a catalyst, or way of getting started: a manual rather than a bible, a map rather than a land-ownership record. A book about writing essays is in some respects like a recipe book in cookery. It provides guidance and practical suggestions about how to achieve particular results by blending a range of ingredients in suggested ways into a single, final product. The recipes can then be improvised around, and varied according to taste. This book will not solve your writing problems for you but it should help you to solve them for yourself and to increase your confidence by doing so.

THE EXAMPLES IN THIS BOOK

The chapters which follow are illustrated with examples taken from essays written by our students. We are grateful to them for their permission to use work which is unfinished and in some cases a first draft (exactly the properties which makes it useful for our purposes); we have also learned from their explanations about why they chose to write as they did. Many errors remain in the examples we quote: learn from them, but (of course) don't imitate them; for reasons of space and continuity, we only comment on aspects of the extracts which are relevant to the particular topic under discussion.

WHO THIS BOOK IS FOR

The examples which follow are taken from a range of sources: school 'A' level essays, undergraduate coursework essays and examination scripts, and postgraduate research work (MA, MPhil, MLitt and PhD dissertations). Some of the writers are native speakers of English; others are not (so-called 'non-native speakers' of English). This is a wide range of examples, involving different tasks and different levels of expectation. But that range relates to our view that the same basic problems in writing literary essays are faced at every level. Much of what we say should therefore be relevant whether you are preparing to write a short examination essay or a PhD thesis. Although some issues we discuss are specific to one kind of work, it should still be possible to take skills you learn from one type of writing task and adapt them to another. The frequent overlap between the different sorts of work you may do – for example between coursework essays and examination answers – emphasises that there are benefits in seeing writing in literary studies as a collection of interlocking but different kinds of work, not just one type of writing that is defined by being 'about literature'.

This book started, for us, with the recognition of two difficulties. One is the range of reactions, from frustration to depression, experienced by many students of literature when contemplating a blank page or an essay deadline. The second is the pervasive underachievement of students who read and discuss works in interesting and original ways, but whose written work makes little impression on assessors or examiners who are not personally acquainted with the writer. This book is for those readers and writers. Whatever success it has will come from the ways in which such writers finally go beyond and discard the book, by writing with the confidence that can come from knowing how what you are writing relates to the conventions of the discipline and the expectations of others.

HOW TO USE THIS BOOK

This book has been designed to be used in three ways. First, it can be read **as a whole**, from start to finish; this may be the best way of getting to know its scope and contents, and the various ways it can help you. We suggest that you read through the book in this way, if you can, before the start of your course, or at least as soon as possible after beginning it. Secondly, the book has been designed to be read **in self-sufficient sections**, for use as you actually go through the various stages of composing a piece of written coursework. You may like to keep the book beside you as a source of specific suggestions and advice. Thirdly, the book has been devised to be **enabling rather than prescriptive**. It offers guidance and advice to help you develop your own approach and solutions to the challenge of writing effectively. We hope you will adapt our ideas to fit your own circumstances and experience.

At the end of each of the seven chapters which follow, we summarise, for easy reference, the general principles of essay-writing described in the chapter; and we list specific practical suggestions we have made, with relevant page numbers to enable you to find our discussion of them easily. We also give exercises to help you check your own reactions to what we have suggested. In order that the book may be used creatively – for your own needs and in your own circumstances – we have also provided space for you to make written notes at the ends of the chapters. As well as adding comments and personal checklists, you may wish to supplement our summaries or suggestions, or amend them for your own needs. Finally, the booklist and index offer a way of tracing specific themes across the book and into further reading.

We hope that this book, as well as others we draw attention to, will extend your skill, confidence and pleasure in writing essays, dissertations and theses in literary studies.

CHAPTER ONE

Deciding what to write about, and getting started

1.1 THE PURPOSE OF WRITING ESSAYS

As prescribed coursework, essays in literary studies generally require you to carry out two related tasks. First, they invite you to show that you are familiar with the basic, raw material which makes up the subject – whether this is a work, a series of works, a literary theory, the historical context of an author or what critics have said about something. Secondly, they invite you to show that you can manipulate that basic, raw material to argue a case, in ways consistent with established frameworks of literary-critical debate.

Many students' essays demonstrate that their writers know the relevant material; however, the essays do not demonstrate this knowledge within a coherent or developing argument. Such essays are usually judged to be lacking a necessary dimension for achieving high marks. So the second task of essay-writing – arguing a case – is important. But what does 'arguing a case' mean for a literary studies essay?

Much of this book is devoted to showing in detail what 'arguing a case' means in literary studies; and the notion of 'argument' will recur in the chapters which follow. Here we need only to establish a rough and preliminary guide. Arguing a case involves the following four stages:

- identifying a problem or issue in a given area;
- establishing competing points of view associated with the issue identified;
- presenting evidence in support of and against various positions which might be taken up with regard to the issue;
- reaching a conclusion consistent with the evidence and arguments you have presented.

It is the fundamental skills of problem-identification, analysis and debate which are usually perceived by examiners and potential employers as the main achievement of literary studies. The persuasive and analytic skills you develop are applied during your course to literary works and issues; but they have the additional value that they are potentially transferable to other problems and circumstances. Alongside the development of these skills, the subject matter of your essays offers an additional benefit. Because it is concerned with questions of meaning, social behaviour and structure, and problems of cultural value, it directs you not only towards a wide range of examples of writing but also towards a greater awareness of moral and social questions underlying the techniques through which analysis and persuasion are achieved.

Once this basic way of tackling literary studies is clear, many of the more specific problems facing you as you answer an exam question or devise an essay topic will begin to fall into place. With the larger objectives slightly clearer, what you have to do is to work out how these are achievable in terms of the wide array of topics presented to you, or in terms of possible topics you are invited to define for yourself.

1.2 WHAT SORTS OF TOPICS YOU MIGHT CHOOSE

In most cases, when you write an essay you largely decide for yourself what to write about. Even where you have to answer set questions – as in an exam – a choice between alternatives usually has to be made; and not only do you have to pick a particular question to answer, but you also have to decide exactly what it is that the question is asking you to do. In deciding what a question involves, you need first to identify where it fits into the range of ESSAY GENRES (or 'essay idioms') which are defined by the conventions of literary studies as a discipline. Once you can identify where it fits, you have a general framework in which to tackle it – or which you can challenge if you wish to. We begin this chapter, accordingly, by looking at the different types of literary essay it is possible to write, considering first the variety of focus they give to their subject matter and the different modes of argument they adopt.

A literature essay always has a *focus* for its subject matter (e.g. on the novels of Angela Carter, the role of 'fool' characters in drama, or the origins of free verse), and it also uses a particular *mode of argument* (e.g. stylistic analysis, contrast and comparison, or historical contextualisation). To begin with, then, we need to identify the different kinds of focus and modes of argument that are possible, so that you can gain a general sense of the elements which are combined together in an essay in literary studies.

focus (i): Authors

> *examples* 'The life and works of Edgar Allen Poe'; 'women Romantic poets'.

focus (ii): Texts

> *examples* Coleridge's 'Kubla Khan'; Ralph Ellison's *Invisible Man;* poems by Sylvia Plath.

focus (iii): Generic groupings of texts

> *examples* The sonnet; eighteenth-century pastoral poetry; kitchen-sink drama.

focus (iv): Historical issues relating to a selected text or group of texts:

> *examples* The specifically nineteenth-century idea of beauty in the nineteenth-century novel; developments in the theatre immediately before the English Civil War; representations of industrial life in early twentieth-century novels.

focus (v): Theoretical issues relating to literary study:

> *examples* Comparison of post-structuralist approaches to the lyric poem; the mental processes involved in construing a metaphor; why it is possible to have manipulations of point-of-view in narrative.

Consider now the various kinds of argument which can be used in approaching these points of focus in your material and making something new and interesting from them:

mode of argument (a): Revalue a reputation (or assess relative achievement);

> *example* An extended essay which argues that Josephine Tey is a major Scottish writer, and that she has been neglected because she wrote detective fiction.

mode of argument (b): Analyse style: comment on aspects of the language of a text.

> *example* An essay pointing out that Shakespeare's first sonnet ends with a comma in the first printed edition and arguing that this is because it is the first part of a larger poem including also the second sonnet.

mode of argument (c): Relate a text to the historical circumstances which produced it, or in which it is read.

> *example* A dissertation which looks at the relation between the spread of tourism in the countryside in the eighteenth century and the development of a new style of 'countryside' poetry as exemplified in Wordsworth and Coleridge's *Lyrical Ballads* published near the end of that century.

mode of argument (d): Place a text in a literary or aesthetic context (e.g. in a tradition, in the emergence of a new form or style).

> *example* A thesis arguing that Robert Louis Stevenson should be understood as an early example of twentieth-century Modernism rather than as a late example of nineteenth-century Realism.

mode of argument (e): Describe or interpret (or reinterpret) a text. For example, you could interpret the meanings of events in a narrative, starting with a description of what happens at an apparently realistic level, then interpreting the events as having an alternative, symbolic meaning. Description and/or interpretation includes some of the kinds of activity involved in an exercise called 'Practical Criticism', which entails commenting on prose passages and poems.

> *example* An essay which describes the narrative of Alasdair Gray's novel *Lanark* and interprets it as a symbolic representation of the state of contemporary Scotland.

mode of argument (f): Take sides in an ongoing critical argument between differing viewpoints. Summarise the different cases made in a controversy, then conclude by taking one side or another. Since critical controversies can surround virtually any aspect of a text or movement, essays along these lines can take many forms.

> *example* A thesis which investigates made-up words (which resemble slips of the tongue) in Joyce's *Finnegans Wake*, compares literary theoretical approaches with experimental psychological approaches, and concludes that the psychological approaches undermine the validity of the literary theoretical approaches.

mode of argument (g): Exemplify theories, terms or approaches, or use a classificatory system to describe a text (usually in order to reflect back on how suitable or effective the descriptive system is).

> *example* An essay showing that the linguistic theory of Conversational Analysis can help us understand how characters in Conrad's novels control each other through the ways they interact in speech.

A simple combination of a selected focus with one of the modes of argument outlined above would be an essay with a focus on Ralph Ellison's *Invisible Man* [focus (ii)], which argues that it is underrated as a novel and indicates why it should be seen as a greater achievement [mode of argument (a)]. More than one focus can be adopted in any given essay, and different modes of argument can be combined; the evaluation of *Invisible Man* could involve a stylistic argument, so combining mode of argument (a) and mode of argument (b). But while a single essay might draw in this way on more than one perspective, it is important to establish which is the primary or organising mode of argument and what is the primary focus around which an essay is based. Otherwise you may obscure the development of your essay by failing to distinguish its overall direction. Many essays suffer from exactly this problem: they lack a clear sense of what the main issues are which are being addressed. Other essays are damaged by what appears to be an opposite problem, but is actually a result of the same lack of structure: they read as if they are trying to solve two or more problems at once.

1.3   RESPONDING TO SET QUESTIONS

If you have to devise your own topic, you can do so by selecting and combining from the lists of different approaches above. But even when you are constrained by having to answer a question set for you, it is useful to bear in mind the range of possible essay genres, so that you can decide exactly which combination of focus and mode of argument you are required to adopt. Finding an appropriate form in which to present your argument is a major part of the process of writing an essay, and our aim in these sections is to help you develop strategies for making sure that your essay has a directed and coherent structure.

Coursework and examination questions are an idiom in themselves. The idiom is worth learning to understand in order to develop a sense of how you should respond to the (often hidden) questions *inside* an examination or coursework question. Here are some words which are commonly used in essay and exam questions, grouped according to the basic types of writing which they might be asking you to do.

TYPE OF QUESTION	WORDS TO LOOK FOR / WHAT TO DO
(1) *comparison*	compare, contrast
(2) *debate*	comment on, write on, discuss (often following a quotation, either attributed to an author – usually a critic – or made up by the examiners)

(3) *exemplification*	illustrate, give examples
(4) *description*	outline, sketch, summarise
(5) *analysis*	explain, consider the implications of, analyse, do you agree with the assertion that . . ., in what ways does . . .,
(6) *classification*	differentiate, classify, describe the types of
(7) *evaluation*	assess, justify, to what extent?

In this book we will look at the kinds of things you have to do to respond to each type of question. This is partly a matter of writing appropriate sentences, for example, so that you can distinguish your point of view in debate from someone else's. And it is partly a matter of organising paragraphs – how, for example, to organise a comparison. And it is partly a matter of knowing where to find help: how to find examples and how to work out all the possibilities of a classification.

In the meantime, note the following features of the use of the words listed above. The term 'discuss' invites *debate*, where debate means reasoned presentation of arguments for and against a proposition, with a conclusion – no matter how qualified or tentative – reached at the end. Words like 'explain', 'justify' and 'assess' are used to focus your attention on *causation* and *evidence*; you should not only describe what you have read but also offer an analysis of why you take the view of it you do. 'Give examples' (or the related, 'with reference to not less than two texts . . .') invites you to present concrete *illustration,* which should generally include quotation and paraphrase (of episodes or incidents from the text) to support the points you make.

We can accordingly make a general summary of the tasks you are being invited to perform in response to essay questions. You are to discuss a proposition, offering and evaluating arguments with appropriate illustration on different sides; the arguments should lead towards a conclusion which (1) follows the arguments you have offered, and (2) matches the balance of possibilities which you argued for in your essay.

1.4 EXAM QUESTIONS

It is helpful to bear in mind these recurrent instruction words ('discuss', 'assess', etc.) as you contemplate in an examination a list of questions that you have to choose between. But it is also necessary to link up these instruction words with other aspects of questions. So in this section, we look more closely at how whole exam questions (illustrated here from recent University of London examination papers) are structured, before considering some more general exam-room strategies.

There are several different categories of exam questions:

(a) Questions on given passages

How appropriate is the form/style of the following passage?

By what means, stylistic and other, does the author attempt to establish the character of the narrator in the following passage?

Write a critical analysis of the following poem. Diction, rhythm, rhyme and syntax may be of special interest.

Often you will be asked in this sort of question to discuss passages you have not seen before. But since the examination is testing what skills you have developed over time, the passage is likely to be similar in some way to passages which you *have* seen. Sometimes the similarity is hinted at in the question itself; for example, you may have looked at another passage involving characterisation and this will guide you in looking at this one. But while you will usually be expected to remember other pieces you have seen before – and how you analysed them – you should not discuss those other passages in your answer (unless you are explicitly instructed to, which none of the above questions do). Use what you have learned only as background, or as a model; concentrate on isolating suitable phrases or passages for comment, and on drawing general observations from them.

(b) Questions which explicitly invite debate, and the weighing of evidence (these might be called 'to what extent' or 'discuss' questions)

'Bakhtin's dialogic reading can defuse scepticism about the possibility of meaning.' Discuss.

'Feminism involves both the affirmation and the critique of female identity.' Discuss.

To what extent should Heaney's poetry be described and assessed in terms drawn from his own critical essays?

Even if the question doesn't specifically warn you about it, by saying 'to what extent . . .', you should generally find that the answer is not at one end or the other, but somewhere in the middle. And be especially careful with formulations of the kind illustrated in the examples below; do not be misled by a direct interrogative – the answer is never just a long version of 'yes' or 'no':

'Psychoanalytic criticism can merge with other kinds of reading without supplanting them: it can underpin without undermining.'

Have you found this to be so?

Is 'warm-heartedness' an adequate epitome of Dickens's social theory?

Can there be a 'science of the text'?

Some writers on such questions unwisely respond with aggressive disagreement to the proposition being put. Unwisely, because the question doesn't usually involve a genuine opinion, but rather a constructed or quoted one which is being used to provoke reaction. (The examiners are asking you to show that you have a view and can justify it, whatever it is; they are not asking to be attacked for holding the view outlined in the question, which they probably don't hold anyway.)

(c) Other specific types of question

In what ways can Elizabeth Barrett Browning's poetry be regarded as subversive?

With this type of question, be careful not just to make a list. Pay particular attention to the relationship between the different ways you identify, and be as explicit as you can about the connections between them.

Differentiate the mimetic *and/or* dramaturgic procedures used in *two or more* of Shakespeare's last plays.

With this type of question, you are asked to identify and compare. As you do so, try to build up a system of classification, explaining your basis for making distinctions.

Are Shakespeare's last plays more concerned with the absence of families or with absent families?

With such questions, a major task lies in unpacking the word-play, and making clear the distinctions you are drawing from the formulation of the question. You could begin your essay by acknowledging this and continue to work with the definitions throughout the essay, relating the different definitions together in the conclusion.

Consider some of the expressive purposes of the rendition of places in Henry James's work.

This question only asks you to consider 'some' of James's expressive purposes. Words like 'some' in examination questions are there to show that examiners don't think exhaustive answers are possible; any response will be partial. But this does not mean you should limit yourself in how many expressive purposes you discuss. Discuss all the 'expressive purposes' you can think of.

(d) General invitations – but to what?

Write on Jonson's use of location in any *three* of his works.

Write on Milton's humour.

With these apparently vague questions it is necessary to make clear your own interpretation of what 'write' means. Roughly, you can take it as synonymous with 'describe and discuss'. The special difficulty here is that since relatively little essay structure is signalled by the question itself, in your first paragraph you will have to make very clear to your examiner what shape you are imposing on your discussion.

(e) Complex questions

'In natural objects we feel ourselves, or think of ourselves, only by *likenesses* – among men too often by *differences*' (Coleridge). In the light of this statement consider the presentation of the relationship between the self and the world in the work of any *one* writer of the period.

This rather convoluted question fits a particular pattern which it is useful to familiarise yourself with: (a) a quote captures a general perception; then (b) you are asked about some other writer (or invited to select a writer) where it is plausible to think the quote may be relevant; then (c) you are asked to discuss this second writer in the light of the quote. Note that your essay in this case is not centrally concerned with Coleridge; in fact you will almost certainly do less well if you write about Coleridge than if you discuss a different author.

We can sum up this discussion of exam questions with the following pieces of guidance (in Chapter 5, we consider in more detail how you actually *write* the passages which perform the functions we suggest here):

* Write an introductory paragraph, but don't use it as a way to put off answering the question. Instead, use the first paragraph as an opportunity to translate the question into your own words. But don't use the same wording as in the question and don't translate 'word for word'; reformulation and reorganisation will force you to understand the question and show your examiner that you do. Translate technical words into ordinary language wherever possible.
* Where a question seems broad or general, explain how you are interpreting it in order to make it more manageable.
* The question may not tell you to give examples, but you should, and you should show how the examples relate to your answer.
* The question may not directly ask you for a conclusion, but give one anyway.
* Don't talk about yourself or comment on the exam unless you are explicitly asked to.

1.5 EXAM TECHNIQUES AND STRATEGIES

Writing an exam answer is like writing a homework essay question, with some differences which point to strategies you should learn. It is helpful, for example, to look at past questions, bearing in mind that there is usually only a limited range of possible questions which are likely to be asked about any given topic. In the examination itself, divide up the time on the basis of how the marks are likely to be distributed; if you run out of time for your first answer, quickly sketch a conclusion and move on to the next question, so that you have provided at least a general indication of work in *all* the questions. (More marks are typically lost by failing to write one answer altogether than by presenting two or three answers which are slightly weaker than you would have wished.) Keep your paper tidy (for example, by deleting all notes at the end), but don't use correcting fluid to remove errors (it is a sure way of telling your examiner that you want to focus on appearance at the expense of content). By way of general preparation, it can also be useful to prepare material in component prefabricated 'packages' before the exam itself.

When you come to answer an exam question, remember that it is probably asking you to carry out a number of different tasks. Begin by jotting down what you think they are, plus any thoughts this triggers off. This stage resembles planning your essay outline, and could give you your necessary paragraph headings (particularly since an exam essay gives room for only a few paragraphs). The question is now in simpler units which you can address in turn. These might include:

- problems put into the formulation of the question – words which need definition or explanation, for example;
- established views on the issue raised by the question, which you will have learned about in the class or by your own reading;
- examples which you can use to illustrate specific points (list the points which each example illustrates);
- crucial technical terms which you need to introduce (e.g. an appropriate vocabulary for describing the rhyme scheme of a poem);
- historical context which needs to be introduced in order to answer a question about a writer from an earlier period.

Establish in your mind the scope and boundaries of the material which will be relevant, bearing in mind the formulation of the question ('choose *two* plays by Shakespeare', etc.). Divide up the time available for the question, so that your answer, though short, is still properly proportioned.

1.6 DEVISING YOUR OWN TITLE

The titles you choose for essays you devise yourself can, if you want them to, be made closely to resemble the sorts of questions you are set as prescribed essays or in exams. Accordingly, when you have identified the areas in common, and the divergences, between exam questions and essay topics of your own, you can draw appropriately on skills you have learnt in one kind of work while doing another. With this in mind, we now consider some of the distinct characteristics of essay titles.

A title is a statement encapsulating the main points of an argument; in most cases, it could be rewritten in the form of a question that is being answered by your essay. The title

> Undervalued achievement: the contribution of Ralph Ellison's *Invisible Man* to the development of African–American fiction.

could be used for an essay which is an answer to the question

> Assess the contribution made by Ralph Ellison's *Invisible Man* to the development of African–American fiction.

or to the question

> 'The contribution made by Ralph Ellison's *Invisible Man* to the development of African–American fiction is undervalued.' Discuss.

In this way, titles can be the mirror image of examination questions. They are phrases which indicate a topic of interest (i.e. your focus) and at the same time point towards a particular kind of discussion (i.e. your mode of argument). Accordingly, your title needs not only to indicate what the essay will be about, but also the point of view it will adopt concerning whatever it is about. In the example above, the phrase 'Undervalued achievement' does this.

There are certain typical characteristics of the form of essay and dissertation titles which you can build on. Note, for example, the common form 'title plus sub-title':

> The Text and the Reader: Construction of meaning in advertising texts *(title of a Master's thesis)*.

> Marx and Spenser: Elizabeth and the problem of Imperial Power *(draft title of a PhD thesis)*.

The formula here involves the combination of two different styles: a main title, in a verbally adroit, catchy form; and a gloss or explanatory paraphrase, couched in more orthodox academic language. In devising titles, avoid over-florid forms, however, as well as epigraphs (i.e.

quotations placed between the title and the main body of text), since these can make the essay appear to aspire to a grandeur or scale that it cannot in the circumstances fulfil. Such titles and ornamentation can create the effect of bathos, or comic undermining of what you *do* achieve. The same applies to acknowledgements (and other devices common in full-length books) if they are used in short essays. If in doubt, keep it simple.

As possible alternatives to the 'title plus sub-title' pattern, consider whether your own title could be a phrase or sentence. Compare:

> How readers construct the meaning of advertising texts.

> A Marxist analysis of the imperialist politics of Edmund Spenser's *The Faerie Queene*

Simply formulating a title of some sort can be a useful achievement, in that it helps you decide how you want to focus your writing. As you write the essay you may find that the focus shifts, with the result that you end up rejecting the original title and finding a more suitable one. This common experience recommends the approach to writing which says that you should start immediately by writing your ideas down, being prepared to discard them later when your thinking has evolved beyond your early plan. More generally, it illustrates how everything you do – even your choice of a title – is a part of your thinking about your essay, and contributes to its development.

1.7 BEING ORIGINAL

Whatever you write, it should be in some sense original. But 'originality' presents a difficult problem because (unless you are doing advanced research) you are unlikely to be in a position to advance new facts or radically new interpretations, or even to have a wide enough knowledge of what other people have written to be sure that you are not duplicating it.

This is especially likely to be the case with short essays and exam answers, where you clearly cannot be expected to be 'original' in the sense in which a researcher or expert in the field might be expected to be. But you will, nevertheless, be expected to be original in the sense of using your own knowledge and independent judgement to argue an original case. Your case gains its originality from the way in which you compare and weigh the different strengths and weaknesses of existing arguments in relation to the text or texts being discussed, and by choosing different examples from those presented in works you have read or lectures you have attended.

Faced with the challenge of being original in this way, some student writers believe that they should copy or adapt other people's work because it is bound to be of better quality than their own. This is inappropriate for a number of reasons: first, because you are primarily assessed on relative quality ('good for a second-year dissertation') rather than absolute quality; second, because there is no point in simply rewriting someone else's ideas (you might as well submit their original book or article instead); and third, because it underestimates the possibilities of disagreement, adaptation and development which exist in all areas of the field. Homage to the achievement of established authors, expressed in the form of direct copying, is not an accepted mode of writing essays or dissertations in (for example) British universities and colleges.

Therefore, it is important in your essay always to identify what is original and what is not. This is not just a matter of showing that you are not stealing or plagiarising other people's work. At least as important is the process of making explicit the argument structure of your essay. By acknowledging sources, you show the foundations for the speculations or conclusions you yourself are adding. If you simply insert other people's material unacknowledged into your own, another danger arises, too: that your writing becomes structurally incoherent (something we discuss further in Chapter 5, pp. 109–10).

1.8 PLANNING AN ESSAY: FORMAT AND PROPORTION

In order to think ahead about your essay or dissertation you need to consider its overall length and the length of the parts which comprise it. This means making decisions very early on about the contents of the *whole* essay (e.g. by writing an initial synopsis). As in the case of the title, it is of course, possible – and sometimes necessary – to change the synopsis as you progress. You just need something to start you off that can then be modified as you go along.

How much should you write? Below, we indicate some typical essay lengths. (You may find that your course, college or university has rules for upper and lower limits, so check these before you start.)

Unless you are using a word-processor with a word-count facility, there is little point counting every word. An estimate is enough. Work out an average number of words per line and lines per page, and this will give you a typical number of words per page. Multiplying this by the number of pages is enough to show a rough total, which should tally adequately with tutors' estimates and impressions (since they won't count the individual words either).

Number of words	Project type	Number of A4 pages
1,200–1,500	coursework	3–4 handwritten
2,000	essay	5–6 handwritten; 8–10 double-spaced typewritten
5,000	undergraduate project	20–25 double-spaced typewritten
10–15,000	more extended undergraduate dissertation	40–75, double-spaced typewritten
40–50,000	MA thesis	150–200 double-spaced typewritten;
70–90,000	PhD thesis	300–50 double-spaced typewritten

When you have noted the overall length you need to produce, divide this length into suitable proportions for your argument, so that not only will you not run out of space but the essay will have a 'balance' as it develops, with worked-out proportions being given to each stage. This means deciding from the beginning a rough breakdown of the parts of your final essay: to achieve this, you should write an OUTLINE. Then you can assign half a page to an introductory paragraph, one page to the summary of what other people have said, etc. If you have a detailed outline of the structure and proportions, then if the essay becomes too long, you can work out more precisely where deletions need to be made: take out redundant or duplicated examples; cut lists shorter, reduce alternative words offered as glosses, etc. In this way you can shorten your essay without losing its balance or structure (which would happen if you just cut the end, for example).

1.9   GETTING STARTED: OUTLINES AND EARLY DRAFTS

Speculating about your essay is one thing; actually starting to write it is another. If you look at your first blank page and freeze, how do you unfreeze yourself and get started? In this section we look at some ways of doing this, and more generally of getting from the planning stage to the writing stage. There is of course no single correct way; everyone writes differently.

One productive starting point is to break the illusion that writing is a 'gestation' process of waiting for inspiration until the essay forms itself, fully-fledged, in your mind and just needs to be written down. Even in exam situations, there needs to be some initial planning and rough drafting before starting on the main process of composition. But generally it is a good idea to start writing *in some form* as soon as you can. Be willing to do disposable work. Versions which you know you are going to throw away often allow you to experiment in ways that you wouldn't risk in a draft you consider 'final' or 'near final'. By thinking that everything is final – that it must pass your own 'quality control' test – you greatly reduce the likelihood of producing any work at all. Remember that in the production of texts for non-examined purposes (e.g. committee reports, novels, paintings, films), rough versions, sketches and drafts are the norm. So there is no reason why you shouldn't do a rough-cut, followed by a fine-cut, before you start on your final version. This is not necessarily an increase in your workload: drafting and redrafting allows lower-intensity and less stressful work than packing everything into a single and decisive act of composition. It is also useful if someone is prepared to read your rough versions. This need not be your tutor; even someone who knows nothing about the subject can say whether you are making sense.

Break down the process of constructing an essay *into easy small steps*. Make notes, draft paragraphs, keep rewriting short outlines. Each step you take provides scaffolding which will enable you to build the essay a little further. You note your arguments on a piece of paper; they look wrong, so you edit the notes, making them clearer or more coherent. The next day, as you come at the problems with a fresh eye (or at least from a slightly different angle), the notes look wrong again, but this time for slightly different reasons. So you do further editing. The text evolves, through successive steps of minor redrafting rather than through the more mysterious process of gestation, and with less chance of outside events or circumstances making you forget where you have got to.

Make a timetable. Step-by-step writing allows you to do this, and commits you to making progress, even if later you discard what you have done. Bear in mind other commitments when outlining your programme of work (e.g. holidays, weekends, need for rest, etc.). Be realistic from the outset, so that you don't become dismayed by your inability to keep to your own timetable.

As part of the process of writing from the very beginning, and writing in small steps, from the first day you should write down, and keep available, notes consisting of a few sentences on each of the following:

(a) the essay's hypothesis (the claim it is interested in exploring);
(b) the evidence or data you are going to use (the facts, quotes, parallel cases from other texts, etc., that you are in the process of collecting);

(c)   brief statements of your ideas so far;

(d)   in the case of a longer dissertation, the preliminary results of a 'literature search' (a survey of bibliographies to find things to read).

The value of having such materials in brief and physically separate forms is that it is easier to manipulate ideas while they are still in note form than it is once you have written them out in prose. A note-form outline of the essay provides a clear conceptual structure, and offers you an overview, which – when inspected closely – should allow you to assess how coherent it is, and how clearly it moves to your conclusion. Sometimes, it can be useful to write each main point in the argument on a separate card or sheet of paper, and physically reorder them on a table in front of you, joining up the points in your mind with a linking commentary. (How do you get from this point to this? What is it that makes you want to put one point before another?)

Before working on anything else write a one-paragraph SYNOPSIS (a summary of your essay's argument). Keep your synopsis handy all the time you are writing, and edit it periodically (because writing your argument down will probably change it). A useful test is to imagine that you are at a party and someone asks you what you are writing about: your answer will have to be short, coherent and sufficiently interesting to hold the attention of a listener who does not have to listen to you. The best answer you can give in these circumstances should provide the shape for your synopsis.

Remember to *focus*. What is important is that your essay needs to be made up of logical or structural relations between points (e.g. cause and effect, consequence, incompatibility, counter-example), not just of a list. As we suggest in more detail in Chapters 2 and 3, you will be able to find materials more easily and see the best arrangement for them when you have formed a sense of what you are looking for. Most fields are too large to research convincingly, unless you go into them with at least a provisional focus. With a guiding aim, you tend to read with a goal or personal agenda; what you read falls into place, at least relative to a notion of what your interest in the field is, or what perspective you wish to adopt on it. Keep the idea of 'perspective' in mind, since it indicates that for your purposes some materials and pieces of information will appear 'in the foreground'; others are only 'background', further away from your centre of interest. Clearly, you need to use the time you have available to consolidate what is going to be in the foreground – what is central to your essay – rather than in mugging up materials which at best can only ever form marginal elements of the final piece of work.

Finally, consult essays already successfully submitted. Just as you can prepare for an exam by looking at old exam questions, so you can prepare to write a dissertation by looking at previous examples which have been submitted and accepted by your institution. Studying these should ensure that you are not completely ignorant of the scope, length, format and demands of what you are trying to do.

1.10 SOME QUESTIONS TO ASK YOURSELF AS YOU CONSTRUCT AN ESSAY

As you begin to write your outline or first sketch, make each of the two following types of plan:

- a one-page plan describing what you are going to do and the order you intend to do it in (a PROCEDURAL PLAN);
- a one-page plan outlining what your essay should look like when it is finished (a STRUCTURAL PLAN).

If it seems easier, write your plans as simple diagrams, with different parts connected by arrows. It is important, though, to limit the size of the plans (e.g., to less than a page each), so that you keep a simple overview. The structure of your project needs to be visible, almost at a glance.

To decide what should go into these two plans, think your way carefully through the following general questions, which should either suggest fresh ideas to you or else persuade you that your proposed topic is unrealisable.

What are the questions I want to answer?

Try to formulate these as questions rather than just phrases describing an area of interest.

> *example* If you start from an area of interest which is 'Irony in Jane Austen's novel *Emma*', try to work out some questions to ask, such as, 'Do any of the characters in *Emma* deliberately use irony?'; 'Which characters use irony, and which don't?'; 'Is there a distinction between the way men use irony and women use irony in *Emma*?', etc.

What is the main or central question that I wish to address?

A collection of questions will not necessarily give you a coherent focus for your essay, so you need to encapsulate as many as you can in a single basic question.

> *example* Which types of characters in *Emma* use irony and why?

What kinds of answers am I looking for?

Make as full a list as possible of what kinds of answer would be possible (to your main question and also to your other questions), so that you can at least consider candidates that your essay may then reject.

> *example* The question 'Which types of character in *Emma* use irony and why?' is actually two questions. Answering the first part involves classifying characters into types, so it is useful to think of all types which might be relevant in answering the question – male versus female, old versus young, poor versus rich, and as many more as you can think of. Some of these may immediately appear irrelevant, but it is necessary to consider them briefly, if only to rule them out. Answering the second part, 'why?' depends on the answer to the first part. But it is useful anyway to speculate about possible findings and so some possible explanations; the characters who use irony might be similar in type to Austen herself (in class, gender, age); or they might be the characters who function as heroes and heroines in the novels. Each of these answers raises further questions. This is exactly how you can build your essay, as a sequence of questions and answers.

What methods will help me find answers?

Your essay needs to provide evidence or reasons for your point of view. All the time you ought to be asking yourself: 'why should anyone believe what I am writing?' and 'what have I noticed in the text or in background, contextual materials that makes me think this?' Even if your reasoning is self-evident to you, it won't be to other people, who will come at the issue from a slightly (or very) different point of view.

> *example* How can you show your reader that you have made an exhaustive survey of the characters in *Emma* and whether they use irony or not? Drawing up a list of all speaking characters is an obvious start, with a note of pages on which they speak, and to whom. Putting all this into a diagrammatic table might be a good way to gather data so that you can see clearly if there are generalisations. You can put the table into your essay, if the information turns out to be significant.

What books or articles do I already know that address my main question?

Draw up a list, look on the library shelves, and once you have the books in your hands, consult the index and bibliography of each for further ideas.

How can I draw boundaries round, or limit the scope of my chosen field?

Bear in mind that background material expands infinitely, and needs to be closed off somewhere to prevent you becoming submerged in an endless and unfinishable project. Take note, in examinations, of how boundaries are suggested in questions, such as 'with reference to at least two works', or 'with reference to works by at least two authors'. With larger projects, take care not to include everything you are interested in, just to bring it in somewhere.

> *example* Avoid the 'Jane Austen, gender, class, early nineteenth-century society and the development of the novel' type of project, which inevitably lacks a clear focus.

What is the relationship between my central question and current work in this subject area?

It is possible that the question you are asking is different from the sorts of discussion you have encountered in what you have read on the subject. If so, indicate that you recognise this, if possible with an explanation of how. Or it may be that the question you are interested in has been discussed before, but that you want to develop it in a particular way, or to extend it, or to disagree with one of its premises. Again, indicate this, as precisely as possible. Establishing how your work fits into debate in the area is an important function of essay-writing in literary studies; generally speaking, you need to know why and how your work *matters*.

> *example* For the *Emma* essay, you could look in a bibliography for a link between 'irony' and 'Austen' and 'characterisation'; you could scan some collections of essays on Austen or *Emma* for possibly relevant material; similarly you could look in books on irony, in order to see how closely your ideas resemble existing material, and what aspects are original.

Am I sufficiently interested in my question or topic to keep me interested over the necessary time period?

With examination questions you have little choice. But you also have only a little time. Some pieces of work, on the other hand, require a lot of reading and study time during composition; and for these you are likely to produce better work if you choose questions that genuinely interest you, or connect with problems you are in any case interested in outside your literary work, rather than if you feel your work is being done out of obligation or under duress. Be wary, though, of topics involving issues in which you are personally very deeply immersed. If you feel it will be difficult to stand back sufficiently to carry out the sorts of procedures we have discussed in this chapter, then it may be best to avoid them.

> *example* If you have a general political interest in social class, this could support an investigation of class as it relates to characters' use of irony in *Emma*.

What kinds of benefits – personally and as a student – are likely to result from investigating my chosen topic?

Evaluate what contribution the project can make to your grade or course requirement, and also what contribution it can make to your thinking or personal growth.

1.11 SUMMARY, SUGGESTIONS AND EXERCISES

Summary In this chapter, we have suggested that *how* you present the evidence and arguments which make up your case about a problem or issue is at least as important in literary studies as the particular *viewpoint* you adopt, and counts as originality. Exam and essay questions come in a range of identifiable idioms, and there are established conventions for responding to them. Essays need to be constructed, not just written; so time spent on an initial outline establishing an essay's structure prevents problems of shape and proportion when the essay as a whole is written.

Specific suggestions

* If you are stuck for a topic, look at our description of the range of possible points of focus and modes of argument, and construct your essay by choosing and combining these established idioms (pp. 11–12).
* Make sure you have a single basic question you are trying to answer (p. 13).
* Learn the 'language' of examination and set essay questions, so that you know how to 'speak' suitable answers (pp. 15–17).
* Break your essay into parts, in advance of writing it, and continuously update and revise your description of its structure. Decide what proportion of the essay each part requires (pp. 18, 22–4).
* Start to write immediately; use writing as a way of working out what you want to say (pp. 22–4).

* Show your reader clearly the structure of your essay or dissertation (pp. 13, 17).
* Indicate clearly which aspects of your work are original and which are borrowed from already published material (pp. 20–1).

See also pp. 25–8 for a checklist for getting started.

Exercises

(1) Select a novel you have just read. Using our description above (pp. 11–12), construct a brief summary of the main points which would make up an instance of each of the following TYPES of argument about the book:

– stylistic mode (b)
– contextual mode (d)
– evaluation of conflicting critical arguments mode (f)

Compare your three summaries.

(2) Select any *one* of the exam questions we have presented in this chapter. Make a series of paragraph or section headings that you could use in a one-hour exam answer. (You do not need to know much about the topic to do this; you only need to be able to identify what you would *need* to know.) Bear in mind not only the length but also the proportion of your answer, so that each relevant issue in the question is addressed.

(3) Invent a title in two parts (as in section 1.6), making sure that it indicates your attitude to the subject matter. Describe (in a short paragraph) the contents of an essay based around this title and briefly explain how the title captures the key idea(s) of the essay.

(4) Invent a research topic (relate it to one of the subjects you are studying, if you wish), and write a list of specific questions you could ask about it, grouped as in section 1.10.

1.12 YOUR OWN NOTES ON THIS CHAPTER

1.

2.

3.

4.

5.

CHAPTER TWO

Gathering your materials together

As we suggested at the end of Chapter 1, when you write you use – inevitably – what other people have written. For example, in writing an essay on some aspect of Emily Dickinson's poetry, you might use, possibly in order of likelihood:

(a) some poems by Emily Dickinson, which you analyse;
(b) a bibliography (list of books and articles), to find out what has been written by and on this poet;
(c) one or more critical articles on Emily Dickinson;
(d) a biography of the writer;
(e) a dictionary of symbolism, to look up some of the symbols she uses;
(f) a concordance to the works of Emily Dickinson (this is a list of all the words she used, and where she used them).

Each of these sources provides new information that will enrich the ideas you start out with; and the materials you explore will also provide a springboard into completely new ideas, that you are unlikely to have simply by contemplating the poems themselves. This chapter describes some of the sources you might need to look at as you go about your study, how to find them, and how to use them.

2.1 HOW TO CHOOSE A LITERARY TEXT TO WORK ON

We can begin by returning to the question of defining your essay topic. You choose an author; but then you need to decide which text or texts to

31

work on (sometimes which parts of that text or texts), and which version of the texts to choose. If you want to talk about the work of an author, you need to judge how many texts to talk about and how varied your selection needs to be (many authors write in different modes: novels, short stories, poems, diaries and letters, etc). Other choices include: should you pick well-known texts or little-known texts? Should you choose texts which are central to established literary traditions (canonised texts) or texts by marginalised writers? The important element here is the sense of *choice and decision*: the materials you choose actively shape the essay you produce. They are not simply background materials for your preparation, but guide what sort of essay will result.

In some cases choice is governed by teachers or by the exam paper. In other cases it is shaped by personal preference (e.g. you already feel that you have something specific to say on a particular work). In other cases again, your selection is based on an informal research procedure: you choose works you consider *representative* in some respect (e.g. genre, length, typicality of theme); or *well-known* works (which you think need fresh attention); or *little-known or neglected, 'minor'* works (which need discovery or rehabilitation). At this stage the most important consideration is that your choice is consistent with the overall purpose of the essay topic you are proposing.

Once you have chosen your texts (or had them chosen for you), you need to decide how to focus on them. No matter how familiar with literary works you become, you cannot focus equally on all parts of a text (particularly a long text, such as a novel): so you need to decide which parts of it are most worth reading closely and writing about. This varies from novel to novel; but as a general guideline it is usually worth paying particular attention to the beginning and ending (where structural aspects of the novel are often signalled most clearly). With a poem, it is worth spending time thinking about why it has the title it has. Beginnings, endings and titles are sections of texts which usually repay particular study.

Do you need to worry about which version of a text to use? One context in which it makes a difference is when you refer to a text by page or line number; different versions are often different in this respect, so the least you should do is tell your reader which edition you are referring to (which publisher, editor, etc.). You might also try to use an edition which your reader can independently get hold of, so that she or he can check what you say. The other reason for worrying about which version you should use relates to AUTHENTICITY. Some versions of a text convey better than others what the author originally wrote. Even the first printed edition of a text may have been altered by an editor, printer or typesetter. For example, in its first printed version Shakespeare's *Henry V* has a line 'and a table of green fields', which modern editors now think should probably have been 'and he babbled of green fields'. Bowdler's 1818 edition of Shakespeare cut out parts 'unsuitable for ladies'. Amos Tutuola's (Nigerian) novel *The Palm Wine Drinkard* had its idiosyncratic English modified by its British publisher, Faber and Faber. Modern critical editions sometimes also make changes which go against authorial intentions; Keynes's Oxford edition of Blake's poems, for example, changes Blake's invented punctuation system to make it fit with standard rules of punctuation. Each of these versions has its own authenticity; and editorial decisions are interesting in their own right (and merit investigation) for what they tell us about the times when they were made (for example, the Tutuola revisions tell us about British attitudes during the 1960s to the English of non-native speakers).

Usually, however, you will be concerned with getting as close as possible to what the author of the text (not a later editor or printer) wanted it to be. This means that you should be aware of different possible editions of the text. It is useful to distinguish between an original edition, a popular reprint, and a critical edition. The original edition is the text as it was first printed; most contemporary novels for example exist only in original editions. Older texts, however, may exist also in critical editions. A CRITICAL EDITION has a named editor, who tries to make the text the best possible version, and will usually include footnotes or appendices explaining decisions taken about words in the text. Critical editions are often more reliable versions of the text than original editions, since they will correct accidental errors or random editorial decisions in the original editions. Older texts are also reprinted in POPULAR EDITIONS (popular = for ordinary people, generally for non-academic purposes, though in practice often the editions used on courses). A popular edition is a version of a text intended for the general rather than the academic reader. You can tell whether a text you have is a critical or a popular edition by looking at the following features:

- Does it have a note on the text, explaining spelling conventions used, etc.?
- Does it have an introduction by an editor?
- Does it have footnotes or endnotes?
- Is it a numbered part of a multi-volume edition?

If the answer to these questions is 'yes', you have a critical edition. Sometimes a popular edition will be based on a critical edition, making it appropriate for most uses. But you should avoid illustrated 'coffee table' versions or simplified rewritten editions of a text intended for EFL students or children.

You are unlikely always to have access to an authoritative edition. The next best thing is to show that you are aware of the issues that surround a choice of text (some of these will probably be explained in the introductory 'Note on the Text'). If you read with such issues in mind – and how they actively affect what sense you can make of a text – introductory notes often become relevant and interesting in unexpected ways.

2.2 HOW TO CHOOSE CRITICAL ANALYSES TO WORK WITH

Much of what you will need for your study will be in the literary texts you have chosen – especially if you are reading annotated critical editions. But you will probably also want to consult critical analyses of those works, for a range of possible reasons.

Perhaps the major problem in choosing critical texts to read and refer to is whether or not to use specialised student textbooks. There is a distinction in principle between a book which sets out original ideas, and justifies them (a MONOGRAPH), and a book whose primary function is to distil and tell you what other people's ideas are (a TEXTBOOK). Textbooks may of course also include original ideas, so the distinction becomes blurred (especially where a textbook doesn't tell you where it is offering contentious interpretations). But developing entirely new arguments is not usually a textbook's main function.

A formulation of an original idea (e.g. in a monograph) is a PRIMARY SOURCE of that idea; its repetition or paraphrase in a textbook (or in another monograph) is a SECONDARY SOURCE of it. One advantage of secondary sources is that they are often easy to understand; but a problem which can arise is that they may have altered or distorted the original idea. For this reason, it is better to refer at some stage to the primary source of an idea, even if you came across it first in a secondary source. Textbooks are useful (particularly for telling you which primary sources to look for), but you should not have to refer to them very often in writing your final essay or dissertation. Quoting extensively from a textbook in a PhD thesis, for example (especially if you treat it as an authority rather than as something for critical comment) is likely to give the wrong impression: that you are a beginner rather than an expert in your subject.

Think about what you are looking for when you consult a textbook. Are you seeking:

(a) background factual information?
(b) other people's interpretations of what you are reading?
(c) accepted areas for debate (to narrow down what you think you should say, because of what other people have chosen to talk about)?

Your use of information sources needs to be guided by a sense of purpose in your search, as well as by the interest and pleasure of browsing. In the next section we consider some sources of information, as we explore *why* and *how* sources can be useful in your work. Our purpose is not to define a basic library for you, but rather to suggest *kinds* of books which you might look for; and our choice of texts is based primarily on their convenience as illustrations.

2.3 BOOKS WHICH LIST FACTS (DICTIONARIES, ETC.), AND HOW TO USE THEM IN YOUR RESEARCH

In most literary essays your central concern will be to say something about a text; and most of what you need will be there, in the text itself. Since the text provides you with so much material, it may not be obvious why dictionaries, encyclopedias and other books in the reference section of your library can be useful to you. In this section we explain why they can, and list some of the information sources you might want to use. In all cases, remember that the information you find is interesting or valuable only to the extent that you can put it to relevant use in your essay; facts do not come with fixed, off-the-peg significance.

The most obvious example of an information source is a dictionary, which tells you what words mean. Remember that what *you* think a word means is not necessarily what it meant for the writer. It may have had a different meaning in a different place (e.g. 'cot' means a child's bed in British English, but also a bed for adults in Indian English), or at a different time (e.g. 'gentle' used to carry the meaning of 'upper class', as in 'gentry', but which now can be used as an approving description – something like 'sensitive' – of *anyone's* character). Because words change in meaning, it can be particularly useful to use a historical dictionary such as the *Oxford English Dictionary* (OED existing as a multi-volume set, or photographically reduced, or on CD-rom). The full version of this dictionary lists all the meanings a word has had, with quotations to illustrate them. Other dictionaries contain lists of words which have special meanings in literary criticism, such as *The Princeton Encyclopedia of Poetry and Poetics* or *A Handlist of Rhetorical Terms*.

If you are writing about a twentieth-century author and you want ideas about the author or what to say about her or him, you can use the massive reference work published by Gale, *Contemporary Authors* (which lists biographical and bibliographical information, together with other relevant comments) and *Contemporary Literary Criticism*, which is described as 'excerpts from criticism of the works of today's novelists, poets, playwrights and other creative writers'. Some authors will be less well-documented in traditional information sources such as these, for example pre-twentieth-century women authors; and here you may find it useful to use the *Dictionary of British Women Writers*. On the other hand, better known authors may have specialised sources of information associated with them, such as *A D.H. Lawrence Handbook*. And some authors have concordances devoted to them. A CONCORDANCE, as we have said, is a list of all the words used by a particular author, with an indication of where those words are used. You can use it to find a particular place in a text if you know a word used there, or as a way of following up a particular theme, metaphor or symbol. For example, if you look up the word 'wit' in a *Concordance to Congreve*, you will find all the places where the seventeenth-century dramatist Congreve used that word; you can then work out what its particular meaning for Congreve must have been by studying how he uses it.

Sometimes you have access to a text, but not to all the information you would like about it. You may have seen a film, but wish to talk about who did the cinematography or who played a particular character. Once the film credits are over, you have no permanent record. In this case you might use a popular reference work like *Halliwell's Film Guide*, or a journal like *The Monthly Film Bulletin* or *Sight and Sound*. There are also more specialised information sources you might need to use: if you want to know about the readership of a particular contemporary magazine or newspaper, for example (perhaps as part of a study of the relation between ideology and audience) you could use *BRAD* ('British Rate and Data'), which lists advertising rates and audited newspaper and magazine circulations.

Sometimes historical information is useful. If you are working on a twentieth-century subject, you may find it helpful to use the enormous amount of information available about events in the twentieth century, organised by year. If you are writing about Eliot's poem *The Waste Land* (published in 1922) for example, you might consider it relevant to know about other events of that year (or the years when it was being written), and so you could look up 1922 in the index to the London newspaper *The Times* (the poem is set partly in London and was published there). In these indexes you will find information about countries, types of event (e.g. crimes), about the arts (e.g. reviews) and about the subjects and terms of reference of contemporaneous public debate. As well as indexes for many newspapers, there are compendia such as *Keesings Contemporary Archives* ('factual reports on current affairs throughout the world, based on information abstracted from press, broadcasting, official and other sources', published from 1931 onwards).

Sometimes a novel or poem gains some of its meaning by quoting or referring to another text. In these cases, writers may expect their readers instantly to recognise such ALLUSIONS. But there are changes in what readers know automatically, even leaving aside questions of education, social background, gender, ethnicity or age. A person in 1990 will have a different store of knowledge from a person in 1890, and even more different from a person in 1790. So information sources can stand in for what we do not automatically know. If you suspect a text is quoting another text, you can check by looking up what you take to be the key word of the quotation in a *Dictionary of Quotations*. If you think an allusion is being made to a Greek or Roman myth, you can try *Lemprière's Classical Dictionary* or some other dictionary of Classical mythology. If you think a reference is being made to the Bible, you can use a concordance to the Bible. In many cases some of the work has been done for you by previous scholars; so, for example there is a book called *Allusions in Ulysses* (which lists allusions made in James Joyce's novel *Ulysses*).

Finally, there are books which have information about many different kinds of topic, and which can often turn out to be useful in unpredictable ways. These include *The Oxford Companion to Literature*, where you will find information about authors, texts, literary movements, and general historical facts. *The Oxford Illustrated History of English Literature* enables you to explore literary history by comparing juxtaposed commentary, quotation and pictures. *The Cambridge Encyclopedia of Language* is a compendium of useful information about language, including language in literature. The original (but still available) *Brewer's Dictionary of Phrase and Fable* is an example of a nineteenth-century collection of somewhat idiosyncratically chosen historical, mythical and literary information; it is useful partly because of its eccentricity, in that it contains information you may not find elsewhere. And it would be wrong to overlook the very large general encyclopedias, such as *The Encyclopedia Britannica*. If, for example, you want to know about punctuation in the seventeenth century, marriage laws in nineteenth-century Canada, the history of the Elizabethan stage, or current theories of myth or symbol, this is one place well worth looking. Ignore the scepticism of those obsessed with 'definitive' sources: the entries in *Britannica* are always good, and surprisingly detailed.

2.4 FINDING MORE TO READ

Besides these almost standard reference sources, you will need to find more specific – and more specialised – ideas about what to read. One way of acquiring such ideas, of course, is to look on the shelves of a library (or bookshop), or in a publisher's or library catalogue, where you will find books gathered by subject and by author. Make yourself open to chance – often you will find things by accident while looking for something else, or when just browsing aimlessly.

You may also like to look in anthologies. For example, the *Oxford Book of Death* will give you short texts relating to death, and selections from longer texts you might want to read all the way through if you are interested in the topic. If your library has a computerised catalogue, you may be able to get a list of all the books held on a particular subject matter. You can do this directly, if the catalogue has subject divisions, or indirectly by looking for all books with a particular word in the title. You could look for all books in the subject area 'feminism', for example, or all books with 'feminism' or 'feminist' in the title. BOOLEAN SEARCH techniques may be available in a computerised catalogue; these enable you to select all the entries which have, for instance, *both* 'feminism' *and* 'Romanticism' in the title (or close variants on these words).

Another approach to finding more to read is to consult a bibliography, a list of books. One place to find such a list is at the back of a monograph or textbook. For most short coursework essays, this may well be enough. But you can also use specialised bibliographies. Many authors have whole bibliographies devoted to them, and there are bibliographies for particular subject areas (for example, *Black British Literature. An Annotated Bibliography*). The most comprehensive bibliography for literary studies is the *Modern Language Association of America [MLA] international bibliography*. Another, more selective and critical bibliography is *The Year's Work in Modern Language Studies*. (Notice that 'Modern Language' in titles usually means literature as well as language, and looking in bibliographies for ideas about what to read is called a LITERATURE SEARCH – 'literature' in this sense means 'the collection of what has been written'.)

A third approach is to look at ABSTRACTS. An abstract is a short summary of content. For example, a yearly volume called *Abstracts of English Studies* gives very short summaries of a large number of articles published in a year; there are indexes to help you find particular topics. *Dissertation Abstracts International* is another collection of abstracts, this time quite long abstracts of PhD dissertations. If you are writing an MA, MPhil, MLitt or PhD dissertation, you should look at this book to see what other people have written about the topic you are working on. You can use abstracts as an indication of something you might want to read, or you can just read and learn from the abstracts themselves.

Another way of finding useful or appropriate things to read is to look at library catalogues which have been published as books. In college and university libraries you will often find catalogues for other collections. These are particularly useful when the collections are subject-specific. For example, there is a published catalogue of the books in the Florida State University 'Shaw Childhood in Poetry collection'; this catalogue lists books of poems relating to childhood, together with lists of poems in the books, and even representative poems from the books – making it a bit like a dictionary of quotations on the topic. If your current interest happens to be in childhood in literature, this catalogue is an interesting place to browse.

Once you start looking, you will probably find more than you have time to read. So you will need to be selective in what you decide to consult. Here are some ways of being selective.

* Choose recent books first (they might tell you what earlier books have said). Check book dates generally, and ask yourself whether a source may actually be giving you an outdated perspective.

* Look at the range of titles in the field and for topics which keep coming up. Make sure you read at least one book on each relevant topic.

* If you have a book or article in your hands, check the contents page and preface or introduction: these will give you a sketch of the book's scope and argument. It is also useful to look at the bibliography or index to see what it includes and what it misses out. (Do the included terms correspond with what is in your view important, or the sense of what is important you have formed from what you have already read?)

* Read the last page of the book or article: with any luck it will summarise what went before, so you can choose whether to read the whole volume.

* Check the contents page and try to link up the entries into a developing narrative or argument.

When you have used a bibliography to find the title of something to read, how do you then get your hands on it? If it is not in your library you may have to use inter-library loan, if this service is available to you. (In Britain all books published are kept in copyright libraries such as the British Library in London, and can in principle be borrowed by your library, though in practice they are not available to everyone.) In some cases, however, the elusive book which you need may in fact be hidden in your own library. (A group of students who were asked to read the poem 'Lycidas' by John Milton couldn't find it because it was 'not in the catalogue'. What they needed to do was to look in *Milton's Collected Poems* or in an anthology such as *The Oxford Book of Seventeenth-Century Verse*, rather than expecting individual titles all to be listed separately in the catalogue.) Finally, anthologies exist for all kinds of text, so sometimes what you need can be found there. This is true even of critical essays: there are anthologies such as those in the Macmillan *Casebook* series or the Longman Critical Readers.

2.5   HOW TO READ A BOOK OR ARTICLE

Finding your book or article is only the beginning, of course. Once you have it in your hands, there are a number of different ways of using it. Because you will often have more to read than you have time for, you need to develop ways of reading more quickly and efficiently. The techniques of scanning and skimming can both be used to gain a rough idea of what an article or book contains, so that you can read parts in more detail if you want to. You can SCAN, which involves just looking quickly at each page, to pick out anything which you recognise as being relevant to you, and which you can then read in detail (scanning involves looking for keywords). Or you can SKIM, which involves just reading the first sentence of every paragraph and anything prominent or highlighted (in this case, it is the general sense and flow of the book you are trying to absorb).

Both of these reading techniques are examples of how reading is a selective activity. Even when you READ INTENSIVELY (that is, you focus on every word) you are still inevitably selective in what you understand or absorb. If you read an article or book twice you will probably be surprised by the many new things you discover the second time. It is a common experience in reading that you read something, then try to write about it; writing about it gives you new ideas, and so when you read the original again you find new things in it because of the new ideas you have brought to it. This suggests that books or articles which are important to your project should be read more than once (early on, and then again later in your study). Reading is an active process, one where what you bring to your reading affects what you get out of it: the more you know, the more you can understand. Don't go to books passively, expecting simply to absorb and to be informed. Constantly ask yourself what key questions reading this book is going to help to answer. As you read through a book or long article, pause after each chapter or section and look back at any notes you have taken. Do they make sense? Do they provide facts or views you can use? Are there particular points you need to go back to, or will need to find out more about?

2.6 HOW TO KEEP NOTES

Your reading will be useful only if you remember it and can do something with it. There are various ways of storing the results of your reading. You can buy the book, and write notes directly on it, or underline (or highlight) parts. You can photocopy relevant sections of the book or article. Alternatively, you can copy out parts of the book into your notes. Or you can try to restate passages of the book in your own words.

Which of these you should do involves the basic decision whether you should copy the original words, or restate the content in your own words. The problem with keeping the original (e.g. as a photocopy, with sections highlighted) is that you haven't really done anything with it yet: you haven't assimilated it or made it your own, in the sense of fitting it with (and so allowing it to affect) your existing thoughts and knowledge. At some point, you will probably have to write out your own version of other people's ideas in the form of paraphrase or summary embedded in your own work; so it could be argued that you should do the rewriting from the outset, as you take your notes, in an effort to get at the ideas behind the words rather than just repeating the words themselves. The problem with this is that in doing so you are taking a risk: perhaps you are misunderstanding what you read, and so your notes become an incorrect version of what was said. One response to this objection, though, is that sooner or later you have to decide what someone means and how it is relevant to you; so you might as well take that decision consciously, while you have the book or article in front of you to check.

However you make them, your notes are a record of what you have read. They may also be a record of your developing ideas. But you need to make sure you can find things again when you need them. This is one reason why cards (INDEX CARDS) are popular as a format for keeping notes. Index cards are easily handled and shuffled; they can be kept in alphabetised boxes, come in different colours, and can have a topic, keyword or reference written at the top, as an indication of what is on the card. These features make index cards easy to organise, and well-organised notes mean that you can find information more easily. One basic decision you have to make is whether to index a card by writing at the top of the card a theme/keyword or a name of an author/title. You might for example have a card on the theme/keyword 'the sublime', including notes drawn from a number of different books. Or a card which contains only notes from Monk's book *The Sublime: a Study of Critical Theories in Eighteenth-Century England*. In general, the former method of organising by themes and keywords involves you more in doing analysis and thinking at the moment of reading, which is generally a good idea.

You may also be able to store your notes on the equivalent of index cards on a computer (in a database, or in word-processing document files). Finding information in computerised notes is in principle much more efficient because you can search for every use of a particular word throughout your notes. On the other hand, on a computer screen you can only see a small amount of information at any given time, whereas with index cards you can lay them out across a table or on the floor for an overview. You also have to be able to have the computer with you when you take the notes, which is not always easy to arrange.

In whatever format you keep them, the notes you make need to be clear; if they are not self-explanatory at the time you write them, they are unlikely to be intelligible later, when your memory of working on the particular book or topic has faded. So read over your notes once you have made them, and edit them until they are as comprehensible as possible without reference back to the source work. It is also generally a good idea to keep your notes short; while you may want to keep a record of everything that might prove useful, your notes will seem unhelpful if you feel swamped with redundant information when you come to refer to them later.

2.7 KEEPING A RECORD OF WHERE YOU FOUND SOMETHING

At the beginning of this chapter, we suggested that when you write you use what other people have written. One of the conventions of research – which we discuss in more detail below, in Chapter 5 – is that you must enable your reader to find again what you have read (and in any case, it is useful for *you* to be able to find again what you have read). So you need to write down enough details of a book or article, or any other source, to enable it to be found again. In some cases it can be difficult or even impossible to find texts again (for example if the text is a lecture, or a television programme), but you should still keep details of them as fully as possible, so that your reader knows exactly where ideas or words come from.

The information you need to keep for everything you read includes the following. (You will find such information usually at the beginning of a book – though some books have details of publication on the last page instead.)

(a) The author's full name. Write the family name first, as this will decide where the work will go in an alphabetical list.

(b) Any other people involved, other than an author. There might for example be an editor, compiler or translator.

(c) The full title – and subtitle – of the work. Put a colon between the title and the subtitle, even if there isn't one in the original. Underline the title of a book, and put an article's title in single quotation marks.

(d) The name of the publisher, the place where it was published, and the date of publication – all for the edition you have in your hands. Often books will have a list of different places; the convention is to choose only the first. In some cases you may want to add further information: books are published in Cambridge England and Cambridge USA, so saying just 'Cambridge' may not be helpful; add country details if you think there is a possibility of confusion.

(e) If the text is an article in a journal or a chapter in an edited book or anthology, keep details about the collection in which you found it; for a journal article, note the volume and issue number, and the page numbers on which the article appears.

(f) Sometimes books or articles exist in several different versions. If you are not using the original version, you should say so (e.g. by noting 'second edition' or 'reprinted version' or 'facsimile'). You should keep details of the original version, if you can find them. For an article in an anthology, for instance, you need to keep details of the journal in which it originally appeared. For a FACSIMILE edition (a photographic reprint of an old book), note both information relating to the current edition and also information relating to the original edition. If a book is a translation, keep information about the original title, publisher, etc.

(g) Usually you will refer to or quote from a particular passage in a book or article; in this case, note the page number. Because literary texts exist in different editions it can be more helpful instead to note the chapter number, act and scene number, line number, etc. (and of course, you should indicate the exact edition you are using). `

(h) For your own benefit, also keep a record of where *you* found the book (which library and the call number), in case you need to consult it again.

There are detailed guidelines, for example in *The MLA Style Manual* or the *MHRA Style Book*, to tell you how to deal with all kinds of complicated cases. Below, in Chapters 5 and 7, we enlarge on what we have said here, as we make suggestions about how to present references in footnotes and booklists appended to your essay or dissertation. But note in the meantime that published rules don't always help you. Often you need to work things out for yourself.

Here is an example of the need to improvise. We wish to refer to an anthology of poetry and prose which we have open in front of us. At the beginning of the book, on the verso (left-hand) page, it says:

Oxford University Press.
London, Edinburgh, Glasgow, New York, Toronto, Melbourne, Cape Town, Bombay
Humphrey Milford, Publisher to the University

On the recto (right-hand) page it says:

A Book of the Sea.
Selected and arranged by Lady Sybil Scott
Oxford. At the Clarendon Press. 1918

The first problem is: how to record the name of the author. Should it be 'Scott, Lady Sybil' or just 'Scott, Sybil'? We would be inclined to use the first, because it gives a better sense of the feel of the anthology; but this is a fairly arbitrary decision, where rule-books do not help. How should we list the author's role? We could say simply '(edited)' but perhaps we should take the title page at its word and say instead '(selection and arrangement)'. Is the publisher Oxford University Press or Humphrey Milford or Clarendon Press? (Actually, it is Oxford University Press, but we can be sure of this only because we already know something about this publisher.) Finally, is the place of publication London (the first in the list under the publisher's name) or Oxford? Again, we choose Oxford, but only because this is usually given as the place of publication for Oxford University Press books. So our notes say:

Scott, Lady Sybil (selection and arrangement), *A Book of the Sea* (Oxford: Oxford University Press, 1918).

Getting to this stage involves some active interpretation (and some fairly random decisions too). As usual in writing, following rules by itself achieves little.

2.8 USING A COMPUTER TO FIND AND STORE INFORMATION

Computers are particularly good for finding, storing and retrieving information. This can be illustrated in the context of literary studies with one or two examples, starting with the advantage of using a computerised library catalogue.

A *non*-computerised library catalogue is likely to be a collection of cards, each a record about a book, in alphabetical order according to the author's family name. If you know just the title but not the author's name, you may be out of luck. In a computerised catalogue, on the other hand, you can in principle search according to any aspect of a record about a book. This is because computerised information is not as rigidly organised in advance, which means that you can search through it in any way you please. Computerised library catalogues are just one example of the many forms of computerised bibliographical information which are available. The *Modern Language Association Bibliography* from 1985 to the present is available on compact disc, so you can do much quicker searches than if you had to haul out each year's book one by one.

Increasingly, literary texts are becoming available in computerised form. For example, the Oxford Text Archive is a collection of computerised texts, each of which you can buy on floppy disc for the price of a printed copy. Shakespeare's works are available on disc from many sources, as is the Bible. Compact discs are available which contain a corpus of a whole century of poetry on a single disc. And it is possible to make new electronic texts by scanning printed texts into a computer. The advantage of having a text in computerised form is that you can find things in it very easily using computerised search techniques, and you can do more complicated searches than you ever could with a printed concordance. Let's say you are interested in the opposition of love and hate in Shakespeare's play *All's Well that Ends Well*. Using a Complete Shakespeare on CD, you can look for all cases where these two words are used within, say, five lines of each other; and you'll get your answer within a minute or so.

Another useful resource is offered by the possibility of putting very large dictionaries onto a single compact disc. The full *Oxford English Dictionary* is available on compact disc; and with it you can do far more extensive searches for information than the printed book allows. For example, if you are interested in the word 'love', with the book version of the *OED* you can look up 'love' and you will be given definitions and illustrative quotations. In the compact-disc *OED*, on the other hand, you can look for the word 'love' not just in the entry for 'love' but in every entry in the whole dictionary; the search will find 'love' in any quotation anywhere in the entire dictionary. A search of this size is impossible with the printed *OED*, where you are restricted to just those quotations including 'love' which the original editors decided to put into the entry for 'love'.

It is likely that computerized storage and retrieval facilities will take on an increasing importance in literary studies; so it is worth exploring them whenever you can. It should be said, nevertheless, that powerful search techniques, across such large databases, will still only contribute effectively to your essay-writing or research if you maintain a clear sense of what you are looking for and why – a guiding principle which is itself independent of the technology.

2.9   USING YOUR SUPERVISOR

The role of a supervisor varies, depending on the level of work you are doing and the conventions of supervision for the department you are in. The role will hardly ever be one of telling you what to do; instead, the supervisor reviews what you have done.

This means that as a student who is being supervised it is you who have to be proactive rather than reactive. Being proactive means negotiating with your supervisor about what you expect from her or him, instead of just accepting the terms (often not actually made explicit) on which supervision is offered. Prepare questions and an informal agenda for each meeting, so that when it is over you can be certain that – alongside all other new questions which are raised – you have asked or raised all the issues you wanted to. Try to arrange for a written record of what has been agreed for the next meeting, so that you can work to an explicit plan. Take an active role in asking for appointments; most kinds of research benefit from discussion at least every month or so. Do not let the channel of communication with your supervisor close – even if you are behind and would rather not have to face the situation of explaining why. Staying in communication allows for discussion and possible help, whereas losing touch will categorise you only as someone who is failing to meet deadlines.

Always bring something with you to a supervision: ideas which you have written down, an outline of an essay, a text you want to talk about, or a plan of action. Your supervisor's approach and enthusiasm are likely to vary according to how motivated and organised you are. You will get better help if you have outlines and ideas for the supervisor to react to;

experiment with your ideas and see what reactions you get, rather than waiting to produce ideas that you are sure fit in with an established approach. See your supervisor as a *facilitator* or notional 'editor'/adviser of your work, rather than as a teacher who will inform you, or as an authority. Ask for comments on drafts of work you have written, and discuss those comments, even if this means talking about apparently negative judgements on your work so far. Feedback provided by your tutor is supposed to be helpful and constructive ('formative feedback'), and you stand to gain most from having comments clarified – even deciphered – where necessary, and ensuring through discussion that you understand the general perspective from which criticisms or comments are made. It is also useful to carry out your own critical analysis of an essay you have completed. A week or more after writing, you are likely to have sufficient detachment to examine your work as a reader, rather than as its writer. Add a list of your own comments to your tutor's feedback, for future reference.

2.10 PLANNING YOUR TIME

Be realistic about time in your planning. And suit yourself – everyone works differently, and your personal best working patterns may well be different from those other people might expect from you. The aim should be to develop your own potential, not to regulate your working habits to a conventional norm.

Allow for unexpected breaks such as days when libraries are closed, delays while materials arrive through the post, days when you don't feel like working, etc. And create breaks deliberately. For example, you should allow for creating variation in your working patterns. Read for a while, then do some writing or some research browsing in a library; this can reduce the effect of strain or tiredness with long bouts of writing, something which is particularly important for health reasons if you work at a computer.

Remember that finishing off (e.g. by adding footnotes or bibliographic references) always takes longer than you anticipate, so allow enough time for this. Be careful with deadlines: some are notional (and extensions are possible); others are fixed and absolute, with the result that non-completion on schedule can mean failure. Check the rules to find out which of these your deadline is.

2.11   SUMMARY, SUGGESTIONS AND EXERCISES

Summary In this chapter we have shown how writing an essay depends on the manipulation of raw materials collected for the purpose, including editions of literary works, critical essays, information gathered from reference sources and advice sought from teachers or supervisors. The work of writing an essay is greatly reduced if your preparatory stages are carried out thoroughly. This involves deciding what it is you are looking for before you start general reading, and, equally important, assessing why you need to read particular works or sources you intend to consult. Keeping clear and concise notes of what you have read enables you to organise your essay without having to refer constantly back to the original sources. Your notes form a bridge between the works you are studying and the outline and early drafts of the essay you are trying to write.

Specific suggestions

* Decide which parts of a text to focus on particularly (e.g. beginning, ending, title, etc.) (see p. 32).
* Make an informed choice about which version of a text to use; try to use a critical edition (see p. 33).
* Beware of quoting from secondary sources, particularly from textbooks (p. 34).
* Find out what information sources are available to you, and be imaginative in how you use them (see pp. 34–40).
* Look for ideas on the shelves and in the catalogue of your library, in bibliographies, in anthologies and also in bookshops and publishers' catalogues (see p. 38).
* Be open to chance discoveries (see p. 38).
* Don't read everything in the same way (see pp. 39–41).
* Take notes, but don't necessarily copy directly from the original when you do so (see pp. 41–2).
* When you take notes, keep a full record of all sources (see pp. 42–4).
* Use the flexibility of computerised texts and search techniques if you can (see pp. 45–6).
* Take the initiative and negotiate with your supervisor for the most helpful arrangement (see pp. 46–7).
* Vary your working patterns (see p. 47).

Exercises

(1) Choose one literary text which you might work on which is

representative, plus one which is *well-known,* plus one which is *neglected* (see 2.1). Explain why each text might be interesting to work on.

(2) 'Kitchen-sink drama' is a name used for a particular group of plays written in Britain in the late 1950s and 1960s. Look up 'kitchen-sink' in the *Oxford English Dictionary* (second edition), and explain how the entry could help you put together an essay on kitchen-sink drama.

(3) Pick a brief passage from a poem you believe to be famous. Underline what seem to you to be the main or key words in the passage, including all names and any words beginning with capital letters. Look these words up in the *Oxford English Dictionary* (complete version, not the compact or shorter version); in *Brewer's Dictionary of Phrase and Fable*; in the *Concise Oxford Dictionary of English Literature*; in the *Encyclopedia Brittanica*; and in whichever other relevant reference sources are available to you. Now imagine you are an editor, annotating the passage for a student edition. As you add explanatory notes, offer all the help you would hope to find, as a reader, in an annotated edition if you yourself were studying this particular text for the first time.

(4) Pick a work you have recently read or are in the process of reading. Look up, in all the reference works available to you, entries for:

- the author
- the title of the work
- the main characters in the work
- the places referred to
- any dates referred to.

Go through the list, asessing what contributions (if any) each new piece of information makes to your understanding of the work.

(5) Make a sample set of 'notes' on a critical work you have recently read to help with an essay task, laying out your notes in two columns. In the left column, put what you consider to be all the main points made in the book. In the right column, note down all the points which would be relevant to or useful in your essay in particular. Compare the two columns.

(6) Draw up a contract which you think would represent the ideal division of responsibilities between yourself and your supervisor. Discuss it with your supervisor.

2.12   YOUR OWN NOTES ON THIS CHAPTER

1

2

3

4

5

CHAPTER THREE

The form of your argument

When you write an essay what you typically do (put at its simplest) is gather material and then arrange it. In Chapter 2 we looked at sources of information and at how to gather material. In this chapter we focus on how you arrange your gathered material in the form of an argument. In Chapters 4 and 5 we consider in more detail the writing techniques through which you can present to best effect the kinds of argument described here.

3.1 ESSAY TYPES

As we discussed in Chapter 1, the underlying purpose of writing essays in literary studies is to *argue a case*. In achieving this end, essays follow certain general patterns of development and direction, which are definable in terms of the *focus* they give to their subject matter and the different *modes of argument* they adopt. We now consider how the substance of those different sorts of essay is organised and presented, starting with techniques for commenting on a given passage.

Commenting on a given passage

In writing on a given passage – often in response to a general question in a 'Practical Criticism' or 'Commentary and Analysis' course – it can be helpful, in considering what to say, to organise your answer around the following questions:

51

(a) Who is the speaker? What sort of person (or creature) appears to be speaking in the text? How do we know? What words, phrases or markers of attitude indicate this?

(b) Who does the passage seem to be addressing? Who (or what sort of audience) must the implied addressee(s) be, so far as we can tell from the passage itself?

(c) What theme or general issue is the passage concerned with? How far is a specific position or attitude taken towards that theme (which may be anything from a conventional topic, such as lost love, to an apparently unresolvable philosophical question, such as the meaning of life)?

(d) What is the overall function or effect of the passage? Does it seek to persuade, command, inform, satirise, impress, amuse?

(e) How would you describe the style of the passage? Is it colloquial, elevated, ornate, comic, ironic, archaic, conventionally poetic, etc.? Which particular words or phrases indicate this most clearly?

(f) Are there any noticeable changes of mood (or direction in the narrative, if there is one)? Does the passage switch from one style to another, and if so why?

(g) How far is the passage supposed to be realistic? Is it just about what it describes? Or is it representative of something more general? Is it symbolic of a theme or topic that is not itself explicitly mentioned in the passage? Is it allegorical (i.e. each character or event in the passage stands for something else in a parallel story)?

(h) What effect does the passage have on you? And would it be likely to have a significantly different effect on other readers (e.g. readers from a different historical period, different class, different country, different gender or ethnic group, etc.)?

There are many aspects of any given passage to describe besides these. But such a checklist of questions can be a helpful prompt if you are faced with a passage and cannot find a place to start. Beginning with one or more of these questions is likely to carry you into other, new areas of your own.

Analysing and interpreting

Beyond answering basic questions of the kind listed above, the next stage of analysing a text is to investigate its patterning or STRUCTURE. Cases of interesting structure might include a rhyme pattern, an unusually high proportion of adjectives, or a particular type of narrative. Every analysis is also to some extent an interpretation; so if for example you choose to summarise a narrative, you will, by selection and emphasis, be interpreting what the most important incidents and characters are. Analysis and interpretation of structures in a text are useful if you can *make something of them* – if, for instance, you can say something new on the basis of having identified a rhyme pattern.

Typically, you use an analysis or description of a text to claim some kind of connection between the features analysed and something else about the text, such as its meaning, its effect on a reader, how good it is, or its historical origins. In most cases the connection is one between observation (of structure) and response (your interpretation). Without observations, responses are mere impressions. Without responses or interpretation, on the other hand, observations are unworked-out descriptions. In between, there are different strengths of connection between these two aspects of reading, ranging from CAUSATION, through CORRELATION, to COINCIDENCE.

Consider a simple example. You analyse a poem as having an especially regular rhyme scheme; you also find that the poem makes you feel cheerful. You now try to connect these two perceptions, by saying that

(a) the rhyme scheme *causes* the cheerfulness;

or (b) there is a relationship between the rhyme scheme and the cheerfulness, but it is one of *correlation*;

or (c) the regular rhyme scheme is connected with the cheerfulness because they are *both caused by something else* (such as the genre or subject matter of the poem, perhaps);

or (d) there is in your view no relationship between the rhyme scheme and the feeling, and they *coincide* without there being a causal or correlative relation between them.

Coincidence is the least interesting of the three relationships; it is also the most common. Causation, conversely, is likely to be the most interesting, but it is also the most difficult to demonstrate. This is because, with a literary text, what is caused is often inside your head: an emotional response or an impression of meaning. While such states are central to literary studies, it is difficult to describe them precisely or effectively; and for this reason, although they are of great interest, they are also inevitably weak points in your argumentation.

Descriptive essays

Not all essays are discussions (or analyses) of individual, given passages. In the case of more general or abstract essays (on whole works, on authors or on critical issues), it is necessary to find other means of organising an argument – though some of the means also turn out to be applicable when looking at individual passages.

The simplest form of general essay organisation involves just the presentation of a sequential commentary or description. But what gives us the sequence? One common sequence is chronology (e.g. the development of a novelist's concerns throughout her lifetime). But there are other kinds of sequence, too, such as a text-by-text commentary on works in a collection (e.g. *Lyrical Ballads*); or you might recount events in a narrative, telling your reader the story in the order in which it happens.

There is, however, a difficulty with the mode of organisation which follows an already existing sequence: it lacks anything by way of your own analysis or commentary. The materials you have collected together (the events in the story, the biography of an author, etc.) are simply presented in the same order in which they originally occur; and this generally produces uninteresting and unoriginal essays. Essays which describe their material sequentially in a list-form resemble commentaries on prescribed passages which work through the text line by line. The problem in both cases is that no process of reworking, assimilation or re-presentation has taken place: there is little *added* by you.

Using the same information available for a sequential description, however, it is possible to organise an essay in more interesting ways. You can demonstrate a process of reordering, and so your own contribution, by reshaping the material around an overall organizing principle or generalisation. For example, a classificatory system imposed on the material divides it into abstract categories (e.g. into a chronology on the basis of definable periods; or into a typology, or system of sorting on the basis of formal likeness and difference). Any classificatory system you use to organise your essay has to be explained, of course (e.g. divisions between historical periods need to be discussed and justified). But introducing a classificatory element almost always radically improves a descriptive essay. It enables you to get straight into analysis and debate, leaving basic description to passages of supporting illustration; and it emphasises your point of view or commentary rather than mere repetition of materials possibly already available to your reader in their original form. (Always ask yourself: why should anyone read my essay, when they could read the original?)

One fruitful form of classification starts from a keyword (sometimes a historical term such as 'Restoration'; a conceptual term such as 'nature'; or a genre term such as 'tragedy'). Consider the case of tragedy. If you are writing on this topic you can work out a list of different sorts of tragedy. This prompts you to do something else, namely to work out the relationship between the parts of the list: why all the different sorts of tragedy are all called tragedy, what the historical sequence and links between them are, etc.

Classification is also useful when you are working with a text which has not been extensively discussed, but which relates to classifications which *have* been discussed. For example, if you choose to write an essay on the novel *A Very Quiet Street* by the contemporary Glasgow author Frank Kuppner, you may not find it easy to get any critical work either on the book itself or on this writer (since no books may have been written about him). But you can work out how Kuppner's novel would fit into various classificatory systems, and then discuss the novel from this point of view. You can try to work out whether it is autobiography or murder mystery and how it works within these genre classifications. Or you can classify the novel according to where it was written, 'West of Scotland', and think about it as an example of writing from this locality.

Classifications are often a basis for finding correlations. As an illustration of this, consider the following project:

> *An essay on metaphors used in advertisements* This imaginary project might begin with an analysis of the metaphors used in ten advertisements. We decide to look for a connection between types of advert and types of metaphor. In order to do this, we classify the adverts into types 'aimed at women' and 'aimed at men' (we could instead have classified them as 'television' versus 'magazine' or 'Italian' versus 'British', etc.; and if our first attempt to classify gets us nowhere we might try one or more of these alternatives at a later stage). We then also classify the metaphors into types: 'metaphors where an object is treated like a part of a body' and 'other types of metaphor'. We are now in a position to ask whether one type of advert typically uses one type of metaphor. If the answer is 'yes', then we have learnt something (a correlation, which may turn out to be an instance of causation); and in writing it down we will be saying something new. If, on the other hand, the answer is 'no', then we eliminate this line of enquiry, and perhaps try one of the alternative classifications of adverts and metaphors we suggested above.

Argumentative essays

In this mode of organising an essay, you divide the issue you are addressing into conflicting positions, or points of view, or sides of an argument. So the structure of the essay becomes a comparison of claims made from differing viewpoints, assessing the validity and appropriateness of each.

Sometimes you can organise your essay around an already existing critical controversy (e.g. between established schools of thought, such as 'New Criticism' and 'Post-structuralism'). In order to accentuate the general significance of your arguments, it can be helpful to generalise from individuals to movements, or types of thought (you discuss Leavisism, for instance, rather than Leavis's work in particular). In presenting ideas of the school or movement, however, you will need to be careful about distinguishing your own words from your paraphrase of the positions you are representing. Be explicit at the point where you leave off summarising and your own words take over (see below, Chapter 5, pp. 105–7, for techniques which enable you to do this). You will also need, in this type of essay, to signal that you are aware of the dangers of reductionism: that is, of simplifying the work of a school or movement until it no longer adequately represents what anyone associated with it would recognise or subscribe to.

Experimenting

A literary experiment changes a text and looks at how the change affects a reader. For example, you choose a narrative, then imagine a different ending for it, and think what implications this would have. Such an 'experiment in your head' focuses on the writer's actual decision about an ending, but also begins to tell you about how endings work in general. As in this simple mental experiment of the narrative ending, most experiments in literary studies involve taking related versions of a text and seeing what effects on a reader the differences between them have. The selected texts (or versions of a single text) will be alike in many respects, yet different in perhaps just one basic way – called the VARIABLE. You are likely to be looking for the relation between the variable part of the text (called the INDEPENDENT VARIABLE because you are manipulating it by making changes) and the variation in the response of the reader (called the DEPENDENT VARIABLE, because it depends on the variation, or changes, made to the text). One of the crucial rules about doing an experiment is to report it fully, so that it can be repeated if necessary. You also need to control the circumstances in which you conduct the experiment, in order to eliminate, as far as possible, conflicting or distracting variables (such as tiredness, lateness in the day, unequal difficulty of the texts used, etc.).

If your experiment involves other people (e.g. if you are comparing different readers' responses), you need to consider ethical issues which arise, including (a) getting their permission to use the results; (b) showing them the results and explaining them; (c) not using their names when you report the experiment (even if they have given permission for this, there is unlikely to be any point); (d) the ethical problem that sometimes an experiment is best conducted if the test subjects don't know what it is for; that is, if there is a 'secret agenda'. If your experiment involves large groups of informants, then you also need to think about the significance of numerical results you may produce; and for this, guidebooks about experimentation and the use of statistics may be needed (see sections 1 and 4 of the Booklist for suggestions).

Providing contexts for texts

Another form of argument to be considered involves analysis of what else was happening at the time a text was written and first published. You can begin to find this out by using an ANNALS, which functions as a short-cut summary of historical facts if you do not know much about a text's historical background. For example, Emily Brontë's novel *Wuthering Heights* was published in 1847; the annals *The Teach Yourself Encyclopedia of Dates and Events* tells us that in 1846 the term 'folk-lore' was coined (which may be relevant to the presence of fairy-tale elements in the novel).

Remember here too the issue of correlation, causation and coincidence. Sometimes a correlation or co-occurrence is incorrectly presented as a causality, for example, by the use of 'therefore' in this sentence:

> Dickens and Thackeray were concerned with demanding social justice in an attempt to make life better, therefore their literature adopted realism as a method.

There could be a causal link between demanding social justice and realism as a method, but it is not shown. There may be merely a less direct link. It might be, for example, that these authors' social concerns and their use of realism both come from a common source: increased knowledge of social reality as a result of sociological work in the nineteenth century and the urbanisation of Britain; that is, a correlation rather than a causation.

Comparing texts

Because a text always relates historically to other texts, one way of developing material for your essay is to compare texts. Texts are sometimes altered editorially for particular purposes, and in this respect, for example, you could compare Shakespeare's play *Henry V* with a version of the play revised for performance in the eighteenth century. Such a comparison would tell you about changes in language and in aesthetics, about the demands of performance in the eighteenth century, and about changes in social values. Even if you have no interest in the play *Henry V* itself, the comparison helps you to learn about eighteenth-century attitudes, by providing information and insights you can then use to look at eighteenth-century drama generally.

Another type of comparison arises from the fact that literary texts often adapt other sorts of text. You might compare, for instance, a real letter from 1740 with one of the letters in Richardson's novel *Pamela* (published 1740, and made up of a sequence of imitation letters). From this you might learn about Richardson's method of writing, as well as about differences between writing which is really private compared to writing which only pretends to be private. Or you could use a text which has been translated from one medium into another. By comparing the film *Apocalypse Now* (1978) with the story on which it is based – Joseph Conrad's 'Heart of Darkness' (1902) – you might gain ideas about differences between film and writing as media, or differences between an early twentieth-century text and a late twentieth-century text; you might also get ideas about narrative by comparing how the two narratives are the same and how they differ.

Finally, a comparison essay always involves a decision about how to organise the comparison. If, for example, you compare the film *Gregory's Girl (GG)* with the play *A Midsummer Night's Dream (MND)*, on which it is partly based, you could organise the comparison as:

> *GG* narrative compared with *MND* narrative; *GG* characterisation compared with *MND* characterisation; etc.; summary of comparison.

Or you could organise the comparison as:

> *GG* narrative, *GG* characterisation; *MND* narrative, *MND* characterisation; etc.; comparison between the two texts.

Generally the first mode – point-by-point argument – is preferable, since it foregrounds comparison rather than description. The second mode of presentation has the damaging tendency to defer argument and analysis until a closing section, before which come extended passages of paraphrase and basic description. Finally, remember that point-by-point comparisons can become tedious if extended too far; a formal analysis always needs to be subordinated to some more general point you want to make.

Using a definition or the history of a word in an argument

An argument can sometimes be built around the definition of a word. Consider, for example, an essay on 'Islamic elements in Byron's poetry'.

One thing you might want to do as a way of putting an argument together would be to look up the word 'Romanticism' in the dictionary, since Byron's poetry belongs to this literary movement. You will probably find that there are several competing definitions, together with examples which will help you think about Romanticism. On the basis of the definitions you find, you could even construct your own definition of Romanticism which would help give direction to your essay. You might for example define Romanticism as 'an artistic movement centrally concerned with the relationship between the self and others'. The next step would be to explore whether the 'others' could be represented in Byron's poetry by people who follow the religion of Islam.

'Romanticism' would be a KEYWORD for this essay. Another keyword might be 'Islamic'. Many words have a history which reflects the history of ideas and the history of society. One way of finding material for your essay is to look up your keyword in sources concerned with the social history of language and ideas, such as the *OED* or Raymond Williams's *Keywords*. The *OED* for example tells you that the word 'Islam' was first used in English in a poem by Shelley, six years before Byron's death. If you now find and read Shelley's poem, you gain the possibility of comparing Byron with Shelley in terms of how they represent Islam. The dictionary entry also suggests that the term 'Islam' was new to English-speaking culture at this time, and prompts you to look up other words, including 'musselman' and 'mohammedan'; reading the entries on these words will give you further clues relating to the representation of Islam in English-speaking cultures, and so further material for your argument.

3.2 ORDERING THE PARTS OF YOUR ARGUMENT

An essay is made up of parts, each part relating to the parts around it, with a forward movement so that what comes first leads to what comes next. Working out the part-structure of your essay is a way of working out what your argument is; and if the organisation of parts is clear, this helps your reader to understand how the essay develops.

Here, for example, is an initial organisation of an essay on the Scottish novelist Josephine Tey:

> introduction
> career as a London playwright
> recent critical appraisal
> powers of description

> humour
> education
> church
> the divided self
> the divided self – most of all as a woman
> her final novel – *The Singing Sands.*

As it stands, this organisation does not make clear how the parts relate to each other, what the development is, or even what the point is of some of the parts (why should there be a special section devoted to her final novel but not the others, for example?). So we might reorganise the parts like this:

> introduction
> biographical details (including career as a London playwright)
> qualities as a writer
>   – powers of description
>   – humour
> themes
>   – education
>   – church
>   – the divided self – most of all as an artistic movement centrally
>   concerned with the relationship between the self and others.
>   – woman (as a theme), and in relation to the divided self
> recent critical appraisal
> conclusion: her final novel – *The Singing Sands.*

Our revised version is the result of the following organisational changes:

(a) We put 'career as a London playwright' into a larger section called 'biographical details', because there are other relevant biographical points we will want to make.

(b) We grouped 'powers of description' and 'humour' in a section called 'qualities as a writer'; we can now add other qualities to this section if we wish. Similarly we have made a group of 'themes'.

(c) We moved 'recent critical appraisal' after our analysis of powers of description and humour because these sections give our own critical appraisal; now, by the time we outline other people's opinions we have something to compare them with, and can therefore do something more interesting than just repeat them.

(d) We have made explicit the reason for focusing on the last novel – we chose it because it acts as a summary of Tey's work, and so is an appropriate topic for a conclusion.

With a longer dissertation, be careful not to overload the first part, especially if it is a biographical summary, a description of historical context, or a literature review – all of which are potentially interminable. To overcome problems of overloading the opening section, try to *avoid* the following structure:

(a) literature review;
(b) introduce case study;
(c) detail of case study;
(d) analysis, findings and conclusion.

In such a structure, (a) usually becomes overloaded. Instead, try something like:

(a) scene-setting; reasons for interest; the problem;
(b) case study;
(c) analysis of findings;
(d) discussion of wider themes; relation to existing work.

In this revised format you present material from your literature review, paradoxically, at the end (under 'relation to existing work'), where you examine implications and applications.

3.3 ASSERTION, JUSTIFICATION AND PRESUPPOSITION

At many points in your essay you will just want to propose or say something; so many of your sentences will be ASSERTIONS. When you make an assertion, what you are doing is telling your reader something you think is true. Assertions can be signalled by writing 'I would suggest', or 'I would argue', but often it is just assumed that whatever you say is your suggestion or argument. In this section, we look at two important questions you should ask about any assertion you make in an essay:

(a) Does the assertion need further justification?
(b) Does the assertion presuppose too much?

We begin with justification. If all your essay consisted of was just a series of assertions, there would be little connection or development between the parts: there would be no argument. An assertion is the basis of an argument when it is combined with a justification:

assertion: 'Dickens showed an incorrect view of the London working classes.'

Justification could be given for this assertion by describing Dickens's view of the London working classes, then describing the view of one or more modern historians, then showing that the two views are significantly different to the extent that Dickens's could be called incorrect. This could be developed further by defending your assertion against an alternative – a Dickens critic who says that Dickens had an accurate view of these matters – and showing that the alternative view is incorrect, or that the critic provides no supporting evidence (and so that there is no reason to believe the alternative view).

While justification of assertions is the motor which drives your essay forwards and builds your argument, you cannot justify each assertion you make. Moreover, how important you think it is to justify your assertions will depend partly on what sort of writing you are engaged in; a film review in a newspaper, for instance, is a genre where few assertions are justified. On the other hand, your reader will be interested in your writing only to the extent that what you say is convincing; and while a film reviewer or a famous literary theorist may be able to rely on their position or fame to guarantee the authority of what they say, you will need to rely on the quality of your argument.

Nevertheless, there are no fixed rules about justifying arguments in literary studies. The conventions about what counts as a convincing argument vary with time and place. Some people think, for example, that value judgements ('this novel is Greene's best') cannot ever be justified; you may disagree – it depends on your ideas about value and whether you think a value judgement is an arbitrary decision on the part of a reader. If you make an assertion which you think in principle could be justified but which you don't have space to justify, you can alert the reader by adding a phrase like; 'I am assuming that   ', 'we could argue that . . .', or 'it is generally accepted that . . .'; the advantage of using these phrases is that you acknowledge that there is some possibility of disagreement.

When you write a sentence, you claim that something is true, that is, you explicitly assert a proposition. If you write 'the second novel Dickens produced was called *Oliver Twist*', then you are explicitly asserting that it is true that the second novel Dickens produced was called Oliver Twist. As you write, however, you inevitably commit yourself not only to propositions you explicitly assert, but also to other propositions which are implicit in, or presupposed by, the words you actually write down. In writing the above sentence, for example, you PRESUPPOSED that Dickens produced a second novel. '*Pre*-suppose' means in effect that you have already supposed or claimed this without needing to write it down. Hidden commitments of this kind are often the result of using particular words (here, 'the') or phrases or constructions.

Consider the following sentence:

William Golding's best novel, *Lord of the Flies*, is a reflection of the widespread pessimism about the morality of children in the 1950s.

This sentence makes a number of claims, some more overt than others. The overt claim is '*Lord of the Flies* is a reflection of the widespread pessimism about the morality of children in the 1950s'. But two other claims are being made as well: '*Lord of the Flies* is William Golding's best novel', and 'There was widespread pessimism about the morality of children in the 1950s'. These two claims are both presupposed by the sentence; that is, the sentence just assumes they are true. Such hidden assertions can easily be discovered, but it is less easy to notice two further presuppositions in the sentence: 'It is possible to evaluate texts (i.e. say that one is the "best")' and 'It is possible for texts to reflect social attitudes'. So what this example shows is that a sentence which seems to contain one assertion can turn out to contain many different assertions, some in the form of presuppositions. This is unavoidable, and occurs all the time as you speak or write. But there is a good reason for making yourself aware of presuppositions: you need to be as conscious as possible of all the assertions you are making, including hidden ones.

Presuppositions and hidden assumptions are the hiding place for common sense and shared assumptions. If you think a particular assumption might reasonably be disagreed with by the reader of your essay you should make that assumption explicit (and then provide some support for it). For these reasons, it is useful to know what the words, phrases and constructions are which regularly conceal presuppositions, so that you know what you are letting yourself in for when you use them.

* We have seen one kind. A phrase like 'the second novel Dickens produced' is not itself a statement of fact, but can be rewritten as a sentence to show its presupposition ('Dickens produced a second novel'). Using 'the' at the beginning of a phrase implies general agreement about the existence of whatever the phrase refers to. A similar mechanism works in:

What is Kristeva's position on gender-positioning in this article?

This presupposes that Kristeva has a position on gender-positioning in this article.

* Other words which carry presuppositions are the adverbial words and phrases which mean 'again' (ITERATIVES):

Emily Brontë began writing the novel *once more*.

This presupposes that Emily Brontë had begun writing the novel before.

* Presuppositions are sometimes embedded with particular verbs, including FACTIVE VERBS like 'regret' or 'know', which presuppose that what is regretted or known is a fact.

   At the end of the book, the main character *regrets* believing in God.

This presupposes that 'the main character believed in God'. There are also IMPLICATIVE VERBS which imply one action by stating another:

   Victorian writers *managed* to persuade us that . . .

This presupposes that Victorian writers *tried* to persuade us that . . .

* Some connectives such as 'although', 'since' and 'because' also conceal presuppositions:

   Because Dickens was a social reformer, he focused in his work on poverty.

This presupposes that Dickens was a social reformer.

* It is also possible to put presuppositions into a sentence by just rearranging the parts, as in the following example (called a CLEFT), based on 'Senecan influence brought blood to Renaissance tragedy':

   It was Senecan influence *which* brought blood to Renaissance tragedy.

This presupposes that *something* brought blood to Renaissance tragedy. A superficially similar rearrangement (called a PSEUDOCLEFT because it looks a bit like a cleft but isn't one) is shown in this example:

   What contemporary novelists *do well* is comment on novel-writing rather than tell stories.

This presupposes that 'contemporary novelists do *something* well.'

* Another arrangement of the sentence which carries a presupposition is the COUNTERFACTUAL CONDITIONAL: 'if X had/hadn't been the case, then Y':

   If Renaissance dramatists *had* not known Seneca, they *would have* been less interested in blood.

This presupposes that 'Renaissance dramatists *did* know Seneca.'

* Finally, another place for presuppositions to hide is in a clause which sets the scene in a sentence; an example is the TEMPORAL CLAUSE, as in the following example:

When Blake saw his first angels he was sitting in his garden.

This presupposes that Blake saw angels.

It is worth checking your essay to make sure that you are not presupposing things which you don't believe are true, and that you aren't hiding anything in a presupposition which needs to be made explicit and justified. But presuppositions are essentially a tool rather than a nuisance – a way of expanding the power of your writing by enabling you to say a lot in a short space. They allow you to imply things without saying them directly, and so to develop complex arguments in relatively short passages of writing.

As you write, there are some ideas which you present as 'given' information; they form an assumed background to what you wish to assert. Presuppositions contribute to that given information. Other ideas are presented as 'new' information: they are what you offer as new, and so of interest. By judging which information to present as given and which to present as new, you establish an important dimension of your relationship with your reader. You are signalling what you take as common or assumed ground between your reader and yourself, and what you are representing as worthy of attention, as 'new' ideas.

Consider this simple introduction to an essay:

> Shakespeare's birth in 1564 marks the beginning of the high period of English drama. When he later produced a series of outstanding tragic works, what he managed to do, in effect, was to bring about the transition from crude medieval drama towards the more sustained literary achievement of the Renaissance.

In this opening, a number of ideas are not stated, but presupposed:

- Shakespeare was born in 1564.
- There was a high period of English drama (which had a beginning).
- Shakespeare produced a series of outstanding tragic works.
- Shakespeare tried to bring about a transition.
- There was a transition from crude medieval drama towards Renaissance drama.
- Other dramatists did not bring about such a transition.
- There is a literary achievement of the Renaissance.
- There was a Renaissance.

All these ideas – each of which is in principle arguable – are compacted into two relatively short sentences and are linked together in a gradually unfolding argument. But the writer could equally have made different decisions about what should be treated as given (shared background knowledge) and what should be presented as new. The essay might have started in any one of the following ways:

(a) 'Arguably there is a transition between . . .'
(b) 'William Shakespeare was born in . . .'
(c) 'The concept of a "Renaissance" in history can be established . . .'

The distinction between given and new information contributes substantially to the level at which your essay is pitched. This, in turn, gives your reader a sense of what sort of debate or discussion you see yourself as being engaged in; and it is this, alongside whatever concrete arguments you make on a given topic, which shapes a reader's or examiner's general response to what you write.

3.4 GENERALISATION

In this chapter so far we have focused on specificities in your argument – the presuppositions in your sentences, the specific things you can say about particular texts, the setting of something in its context, and so on. However, specific observations always needs to be related to general claims or GENERALISATIONS, without which the specific can just seem trivial and random. For example, a specific observation about some aspect of a text (such as its rhyme scheme) could lead to a generalisation based on how it fits with other related observations (the rhyme schemes of other poems by the same poet). A concrete comment on some special element of the text (such as a particularly striking metaphor) could lead to a more abstract general discussion of its significance beyond the text (what makes any metaphor striking?).

Generalising from your experience of reading one unique passage or making a specific concrete observation leads to speculation about patterns or regularities, and beyond this to thinking about causation and correlation, which are central to explanation and argument. So generalisation is important as a way of pulling you out of just describing the details of your individual experience as a reader, enabling you to make statements which are likely to be of interest to others about patterns or structures in the way literary texts work.

In practice, you might, for instance:

(a) Broaden your essay's conclusions, so that they could in principle be applied to other books, or an author's work as a whole.

Example In an essay on an eighteenth-century play, which has argued that the women in the play are generally seen to be a source of disruption or confusion, you could conclude by asking whether women are general sources of disruption, broadly understood, in eighteenth-century drama.

(b) Treat a specific question or topic as an instance of a more general question or topic.

Example The topic 'Islamic elements in Byron's poetry' could be given greater interest and significance by placing it in a more general discussion of 'foreignness' in British Romantic texts.

(c) Try to link together the scattered specific observations you might make on a text.

Example If you have a paragraph on irony in Conrad's 'Heart of Darkness', a paragraph on characterisation and a paragraph on narrative closure, you could try to link them together by talking more generally about the abstract relationship between irony, characterisation and narrative closure.

3.5 SIGNALLING YOUR ATTITUDE TOWARDS YOUR OWN ARGUMENT

As you construct your argument, you will be obliged to make judgements about how firmly you are committed to each of its ideas, and how strong the evidence is for believing them. As you present ideas, therefore, you need to consider issues of EPISTEMIC MODALITY. Epistemic modality (the word 'epistemic' means 'to do with knowledge') involves various markers in language of the degree of certainty or possibility a speaker or writer feels towards what is being said. It includes modal verbs such as 'must' and 'may', as well as phrases such as 'it is possible that . . .', 'it is likely that . . .'. A range of adverbial expressions, including 'apparently' and 'actually', have a similar effect.

Two different problematic situations are likely to arise as you present your argument. The first is that what you say seems obvious; so, in slight embarrassment, you add 'obviously' or 'of course' – implying 'of course everyone knows this'. The second situation is that you feel there is a risk of overstating the line of argument you are pursuing.

Consider first the effect of adding 'of course' to a sentence.

George Eliot of course believed that . . .

If we already know what we are being told – as 'of course' implies – then the question immediately arises why we are being told again. Sometimes 'of course' is added not because the information is obvious, but rather because you want to create the effect of being someone so deeply familiar with the material that this information is basic or obvious. Consider the different impression of yourself which you would give if you wrote:

> Dickens, of course, was a novelist.

As opposed to writing:

> Dickens, of course, completed the last double instalment of *Martin Chuzzlewit* in the middle of June 1844.

As in most other areas of essay writing, there is no fixed rule governing use of 'of course'. What you need to do, in using the expression, is to anticipate what effect its use is likely to have on your probable readers – and act accordingly.

When, on the other hand, a claim you are making looks overstated (possibly unsustainable in its generalised form, or stronger than the evidence you have properly warrants), it is possible to tone down what you are saying by using indicators (HEDGES) that show you recognise the difficulty of certainty in the area. You can replace simple statements of fact or opinion with hedges such as 'it seems likely that . . .', 'this may be . . .', 'it is reasonable to suppose that . . .', and occasionally with 'relatively', 'in effect', 'seemingly' or 'it seems that'. Other useful words here are, 'evidently', 'rather', 'somewhat', 'generally', 'on the whole', 'can appear to' and 'arguably'. Take special care with 'arguably', however. This word works well as a hedge as regards a passing topic (e.g. 'this is arguably also the case in Aphra Behn's other works . . .'). But if you use 'arguably' in the case of a central or major argument you are making, you invite the unspoken response: 'Well, if it's arguable, then let's *hear* the arguments, since this is what the essay is supposed to be about.'

You should also note, in using hedging and qualifying expressions, that they will affect the overall tone or REGISTER of your essay (as we shall examine in the next chapter). They may suggest that you have no confidence in your argument or even that you can't make up your mind – and that does not make for much of an argument.

3.6 SUMMARY, SUGGESTIONS AND EXERCISES

Summary In this chapter, we have described the different forms an argument in literary studies can take. In any argument you develop, we have suggested that it is important to distinguish between views you are taking for granted, views you are directly asserting and views with which you disagree. By signalling clearly the significance of the ideas you present – and the attitude you are adopting towards them – you enable your reader to follow the essay as a coherent and developing debate, in which the generalisations and conclusions you finally draw will seem reasonable and justified.

Specific suggestions

   ★ Remember, writing an essay means arguing a case (see p. 51).

   ★ Begin work by identifying the problems you hope to solve and structure the essay around them (see p. 51).

   ★ Get into the habit of routinely asking a list of questions about any text you have to analyse (see p. 52).

   ★ Analysing the structure of a text is useful only if you can make something of it, such as linking it with something else about the text in a correlation or causal relation (see p. 53).

   ★ Organising an essay around a pre-existing sequence (such as historical order) is straightforward but often not the most interesting or useful option (see p. 54).

   ★ Explore how the text can be understood according to a classificatory system (see pp. 54–5).

   ★ If your essay works by comparing other people's arguments be careful not to be too simplificatory, and clearly indicate the origin of each argument you present (see p. 56).

   ★ Consider modifying a text as an experiment, to see how it works (see p. 56).

   ★ Material for your essay can come from the text's original historical context, or through comparison between texts (see pp. 57–9).

   ★ Start your essay with a statement of the problem you wish to investigate (see p. 61).

   ★ As a way of finding the best structure for your essay, write out all the main points you think you need to make, and rearrange them until they develop as an overall argument (see pp. 59–61).

   ★ Try to draw the general significance out of specific observations (see p. 56).

   ★ It may be better to discuss other people's ideas at the end rather than the beginning of your essay (see pp. 60–1).

   ★ Know your presuppositions (see pp. 62–5).

   ★ Think through the implications of inserting words like 'of course' and 'arguably' (see pp. 67–8).

Exercises

(1)   Find an anthology of poetry, and open it at page 50; take the first poem on that page (all of it, including any part before or after page 50), and answer the eight questions on p. 52, section 3.1.

(2)   Choose a poem (the same one as in exercise 1 if you like), and put the title after the first stanza, so that it is in the middle of the poem instead of at the beginning. You have just changed an independent variable. How does it change the meaning or effect on the text, as far as you as a reader can tell? (This is the dependent variable.) Briefly explain what the result of this experiment tells you about the function of the title in this poem (see p. 56).

(3)   In 1902 the first major science fiction film was made, in France: the twenty-one-minute silent *A Trip to the Moon*, by George Méliès. Look up 1902 in an annals or book of dates and events, and make a list of ten other events or publications (historical, artistic, literary, philosophical, musical, scientific, etc.) from 1902. Discuss how you could refer to some of these events or publications if you had to write an essay on *A Trip to the Moon* in its historical context.

(4)   Pick an essay topic you have recently completed. Using our discussion of essay types above (pp. 53–7), decide which of the following types your essay is:

DESCRIPTIVE	If so, how is it organised: line by line? thematically? etc.
ARGUMENTATIVE	If so, what are the main conflicting positions or theories you are evaluating?
EXPERIMENTAL	If so, what did you actually *do* to provide evidence that might persuade your reader?

Now reconsider the question you were answering. Do you now think the way of organising your essay was in fact the best way of approaching the topic? Assess possible alternatives.

(5)   Pick an essay question (either from our list in Chapter 1, or from work prescribed during your course). List on a piece of paper all the presuppositions you think the title contains (as we have done above, pp. 63–5). Now underline all the presuppositions in your list which seem to you to require justification or refutation, leaving others which you feel are relatively uncontroversial. Now consider those that you did not underline. Is it possible to identify the considerations which lead you to believe that these presuppositions don't need justification or explanation in your essay?

3.7   YOUR OWN NOTES ON THIS CHAPTER

1.

2.

3.

4.

5.

CHAPTER FOUR

Register: the 'voice' you use when you write

So far, we have looked at ways of getting started, at researching your ideas and at how an argument is structured. In the next three chapters we look more closely at the *texture* of essay-writing. In this chapter we consider how you develop an appropriate voice to write in, since this is how a sense of yourself, as the writer, is conveyed. Your 'voice' is achieved in two main ways, and we discuss each in turn: the particular style you adopt and more direct ways of referring to yourself and addressing your reader.

4.1 CHOOSING A REGISTER WHICH GIVES YOU AN APPROPRIATE VOICE

In different situations we write and speak differently. The difference is one of REGISTER. For example, a birthday card greeting is written in a different register from a legal contract in that it uses a different vocabulary, uses a different layout on the page, uses rhyme, etc. To see that this is the case, annotate each term below to say whether it belongs to the typical register of the birthday card or the register of the legal contract (even if you have never seen a legal contract you can probably do this).

vocabulary	henceforth	you're	
punctuation	!	:	
layout	two words on a line	rhyme	numbered page
typeface	small print	big print	

Our choice of register when we write displays our attitude towards our reader and towards the subject matter we are writing about. The choice in this way contributes to the VOICE in which we write ('writing voice' here alludes to the notion of speaking voice, in which we express attitude by intonation, tempo and other means). Imagine, for example, the consequences of writing a birthday card in the register of a legal contract (or vice versa). It is true that such rewriting in unexpected registers has been used by literary writers, particularly in the twentieth century (James Joyce's novel *Ulysses* is a famous example of this); but such experimentation is not a convention of essay-writing in literary studies.

Rather, the convention is that certain registers are used consistently in essays. So it is helpful to understand what such registers consist of and how you create them. It is also useful to see how you can improvise at their boundaries if you wish to. Investigating register should enable you to develop a style that observes established conventions but is at the same time not too disconnected from your own voice or sense of self. In this chapter we consider some norms of style. But it is important to stress from the outset that each norm can (and should) be overruled, for specific purposes of your own.

Initially, however, finding an appropriate register is likely to involve accentuating aspects of what you already see as 'your own voice', perhaps combined with some degree of imitation of one or more voices you like. Imitating the voices of other writers is common in literary criticism. There has been extensive imitation, for example, of the vocabulary and style of the critic F.R. Leavis (e.g. in use of such words as 'equipoise' and 'maturity' to describe writers' qualities, or of such phrases as 'it seems to me that . . .'). More recently, there has been widespread imitation of styles of literary-theoretical writing, much of it read in translation from French (so occasionally incorporating features of French discourse which have survived translation).

These forms of imitation are not surprising. It has always been common for students of literature to imitate their teachers' styles, including in seemingly incidental respects. Such imitation is evident also in traditions (or 'schools') of published criticism, where influence can mean an influence of style as well as of ideas, beliefs or theories. In fact, the two overlap, when certain key words are understood in senses which presume familiarity with the ways they have previously been used. One example of this is the term 'Orientalism', which now has a specialised, polemical meaning, following discussion of the term in Edward Said's book *Orientalism*.

On the whole, when you write you are unlikely to *intend* pastiche (imitative adaptation) or caricature (hostile or critical adaptation). In order to test that you have avoided these, try reading your writing aloud: in general, if you don't feel comfortable saying something aloud, it may be better not to write it. Readers – not only teachers and examiners, but readers generally – develop such sophisticated responses to nuances of register that faked styles are likely to be noticeable. So such styles will probably be ineffective or even counterproductive; and they are also potentially embarrassing to the writer. This is not to say that there is a 'natural' style for you; all styles are constructs, and the question is not one of 'authentic' versus 'faked' but of appropriateness.

4.2   AN ACADEMIC REGISTER

The academic essay or dissertation is a 'situation' which has its own appropriate register. The register of academic writing is influenced by several different factors. For example, certain things conspire to give academic register connotations of 'seriousness': you are being assessed on your writing (a serious matter) and you are writing about important things, such as culture (a serious topic). These connotations of seriousness lead to academic writing having a rather formal register, which is for example different from the register of everyday speech. Register-shifting, while a possibility in certain sorts of text, is discouraged in academic texts because it can often have the effect of ironising your writing, something which is undesirable if you have to demonstrate clearly your knowledge and ideas. Academic register is formal, but not as formal as legal or religious language, with their archaic vocabularies; again the underlying idea that your writing should be clear means that your style can not be too obscure. More generally, the fact that literary studies is sometimes thought of as a general training in thinking and writing means that you are expected to be able to control how you write – in particular, that you are able consistently to use a particular appropriate register.

One of the main characteristics of the register appropriate for academic writing is that it does not resemble the register of conversational speech. Here are some of the features of the register of conversational speech which an academic register avoids:

– contractions like 'there's', 'it's', 'they've', etc. These can be replaced with: 'there is', 'it is', 'they have', etc.
– emphasis, which can be expressed in non-academic writing by italics, capitals or underlining.
– exclamations like 'How awful the line is!' 'What a bad poem this is!' These can be removed altogether, or replaced with statements such as 'in my view this is not a good poem'.

- informal colloquialisms like 'naff', 'OK', 'maybe'. These can be replaced with other more formal terms: 'unsuccessful', 'acceptable', 'perhaps'.

In view of what we have said about the suitability of particular registers for writing, you may be surprised that we ourselves are adopting a relatively conversational register in this book. This is because we hope to establish an informality that we feel will be suitable here, even if it might be inappropriate in degree coursework, in a PhD thesis or in a research monograph. In general this book is written in a register we consider appropriate for a textbook of this type. Textbooks have a register of their own and do not provide a suitable model for imitating in your essay-writing.

In part, academic register is a convention you learn to adopt so that your essays 'sound right'. At least some of the elements, however, have a more important function. While the first of the four examples we have quoted seems relatively trivial, the final two have more significance. Our second and third illustrations express personal response without any justification, explanation or apparent room for argument. In doing so, they replace debate with assertion, and pull an essay away from patterns of reasoned argument.

Overall, most teachers of essay-writing would say that academic register involves clarity and modern usage, coupled with a degree of formality that nevertheless does not extend into pomposity or technical difficulty. If we try to put that description more concretely, we might describe essay-writing as involving a standardised, written variety of language which seeks to communicate clearly while following academic conventions. 'Standardisation' in this context means a restriction imposed on a number of aspects of usage which are nevertheless completely appropriate *in other circumstances.*

A difficult question remains unanswered by the notion of standardisation, however: the status of class, ethnic or regional variation. Consider for example 'didnae' (= 'didn't'). This is a regional variation of 'didn't' used by some Scottish speakers. Because regional variations tend to be more pronounced among working-class speakers, it is also a class variation. Putting it in an academic essay would certainly be unexpected, but it might be possible to claim that it is a regional/class standard written form. One might answer in this case that it is also a typical feature of speech, so should probably be analysed as a contraction and for this reason avoided in academic writing – even if one accepts the idea of a regional/class standard. But now consider the term 'outwith' (= 'outside'). This rather formal term found in Scottish English is often used in academic writing in Scotland, and would seem to be a clear case of dialectal variation between different standard academic registers.

4.3 SENTENCE LENGTH AND SENTENCE COMPLEXITY

One of the major differences between speaking and writing is that speaking relies more on the hearer's memory than writing does. This means that a written sentence can be longer than a spoken sentence. Moreover, written sentences can use punctuation as a way of indicating structure, and so can more easily manage complex constructions. Where a spoken sentence is long and complicated it is more likely to be PARATACTIC; this means it is likely to be a string of sentences tied together with 'and', 'or', or 'but'. A written sentence, on the other hand, can more easily be HYPOTACTIC, which means that it can have complex relations between its parts – one inside another, rather than just one after another.

Academic register is usually characterised partly by avoiding the features of spoken register. Does this therefore mean that you should avoid short sentences? Certainly, there are some extremely short sentences (e.g. 'Yes.' or 'I do.') which can be used only occasionally, for special effect. On the whole, though, relatively short sentences offer the advantage of helping you to keep your writing clear and understandable.

If short and simple sentences dominate your writing, however, it may become monotonous. So you should entertain the possibility of communicating more complex thoughts by building more complex sentences. Consider this extract, which involves a sequence of short sentences (we have added numbers to make the sentences easier to identify):

> (1) Both Brontë and Hardy choose to present their heroine within an organic structure. (2) This reflects their development. (3) Themes of nature and setting are apparent in both novels. (4) They are used in relation to the heroines' development in various ways.

To bring about greater stylistic variation and interest, the extract could be rewritten, by combining sentences (1) and (2), and sentences (3) and (4):

> As a way of reflecting the development of their heroines, both Brontë and Hardy present them within an organic structure. Themes of nature and setting, which are used in relation to the heroines' development in various ways, are apparent in both novels.

It is also possible to combine sentences using semicolons. We could, for example, replace the full stop between the two sentences of our rewritten version with a semicolon, so turning the original four short sentences into a single, more complex sentence. But you do come to a limit with long sentences. A single sentence of more than about four lines puts unreasonable demands on your reader:

Since Etherege (writing in a later period than Wycherley and recognising a greater desire for a new 'Man of Mode') recognises that love, sex and inheritance are still important considerations, which he also criticises, both playwrights can be said to expose hypocrisy rather than improve society, as heroes and heroines are constantly undermined by the contrasts created in the new social order and the codes of morality being set up which are both critical and celebratory.

In particular, it is usually *not* a good idea to expand the length of a sentence by inserting – as in the passage above – a long PARENTHETICAL (i.e. a sentence in brackets or between dashes). Parentheticals can usually be lifted out, and placed either before or after the sentence in which they are embedded, then connected with their original context by a suitable linking expression (for discussion of links between sentences, see Chapter 5, pp. 100–5).

4.4 REGISTER CONSISTENCY

As has been suggested above, there are many different styles of essay-writing. While the influential critic F.R. Leavis adopted in some respects an intimate, conversational tone, writing influenced by Structuralism typically adopts a seemingly more dispassionate, 'objective' scientific voice (e.g. 'at this level the inscribed machinery of fixed subject positions is threatened'). Either of these styles – which here represent different ends of a spectrum – is widely accepted as a norm of academic discourse. But this does not mean that adopting a register is simply a matter of choosing. You need to bear in mind that style links up with more important beliefs about what literary analysis is for (e.g. is it a form of humanistic debate, in which case conventions of gentle persuasion should be observed; or is it investigative research, in which case more rigorous and systematic discourse is required?).

Whatever choice you make stylistically, you need to maintain a register consistently, so that (even though the register is selected and constructed) it appears plausible as a 'genuine' voice rather than merely an unstable, contrived style. Register-drift or register-clash, where forms from one register surface unexpectedly in another, often indicate that a style is not under control. Sometimes, register inconsistency produces unintended pastiche and humour, in the same way that direct imitation of published styles can. Consider this from an essay on the poem 'Marriage' by Marianne Moore:

Moore states her case combining wit and sharp, almost black, humour in attempting to ridicule male vanity in marital union. Marriage is seen as despicable through the force and longevity of the poem. However, she still retains a trademark in the numerous quotes and sources of thought she incorporates into the text, providing ammunition from scholarly sources in proving her point, even if it means twisting what they say to fit her point of view.

Notice here the phrase 'marital union' in the first sentence. This is no doubt used partly to avoid repeating 'marriage', which is the title of the poem and so has already been used more than once. But the phrase used instead ('marital union') introduces another (religious or moral?) register that clashes with the rest of the paragraph. Consider, too, the word 'longevity' in the next sentence. It is difficult to make sense of this word here (since 'longevity' means 'length of life', rather than simply 'length', and is difficult to apply, except metaphorically, to a poem). The effort to produce a technical or elevated alternative to 'length' results here only in a comic effect (a sort of MALAPROPISM, or effect of trying to use words which are imperfectly understood). Finally, consider the word 'quotes' in the third sentence, and the common metaphorical senses of 'trademark' (meaning 'a distinctive feature or characteristic') and 'ammunition' (meaning 'some powerful means of support'); these words introduce an element of informality – especially 'quotes', which is a marked alternative to 'quotations' – which pulls the paragraph in exactly the opposite direction from the upward shift in register sought in 'marital union'. The resulting tension in the register makes the paragraph as a whole inconsistent and slightly comical.

4.5 SIGNALLING ATTITUDE TOWARDS YOUR READER AND TOWARDS WRITERS YOU ARE DISCUSSING

Aspects of your chosen register signal your attitude towards your reader, as well as, sometimes, towards the writer(s) you are discussing. Take care not to condescend to your reader (e.g. 'the reader would do well to consider this point . . .'). Equally, you should try to avoid condescending to, or appearing to patronise, the writer being discussed (e.g. 'Keats is to be congratulated for his use of rhyme . . .').

Because exam questions and essay titles often ask you to judge texts, it can be difficult to avoid such patronising effects. But pointing out limitations in a writer can sometimes seem arrogant, or at least condescending, as in this extract:

At times Eliot is too confusing, too abstract and too well read, but his poems initially only demand a first response or simply an appreciation of the words, their structure, sound and order. Eliot uses at times a simplistic traditional form which incorporates elements of modernism, i.e. the subject matter providing a quirky pattern common in some poems.

Notice in this extract the effect produced by the repeated word 'too', which suggests a slightly dismissive superiority on the part of the writer – an effect reinforced by the words 'simplistic' and 'quirky'.

Usually your criticisms of literature will be based on your experience as a reader, not on your own skills as a literary writer. Accordingly, you can show your reader that your critical judgements are based on what you know has been achieved by other writers you have read (effects which can therefore be compared with each other). In this way, you reduce the impression that you are judging writing by a known literary writer as 'unsuccessful' in direct comparison with your own capabilities or achievements.

4.6 EXPRESSING TASTE AND VALUE

Representing your feelings or responses to a passage can also present register difficulties. Many conventional literary-critical terms for representing feeling can sound dated, affected, or even a parody of literary writing or reviewing: 'forceful', 'affecting', 'tellingly apt', as well as the more neutral (sometimes ironic or euphemistic) 'interesting', 'original', 'thought-provoking', or 'persuasive'.

One alternative to such phrases lies in expressions of your own which are intended to convey more genuine, original response, but which within the overall register of academic essay-writing can sound uncritical or even gushing: 'brilliant', 'fantastic', 'really wonderful', 'quite magical', 'unbelievably beautiful'. The vocabulary of evaluation, especially praise, is so heavily used in speech – including in HYPERBOLE, or exaggerated forms – that it can take on surprising effects in more formal, written contexts. Consider the following, apparently straightforward sentence:

There are many concerns that make the book very interesting indeed.

By surrounding the adjective 'interesting' with two intensifiers – 'very' and 'indeed' – the writer seems to recognise that the word 'interesting' itself is somehow inadequate. In these circumstances, it is better to select a different adjective (or more extended description) in the first place, and so be able to dispense with the 'very' and the 'indeed'.

In literary criticism, statements of praise are conventionally handled in a low-key way, often by slipping in a word which indicates skill, like the italicised adjectives and adverbs in these examples:

> In *Bleak House*, Dickens is *careful* not to represent Chancery as . . .

> Toni Morrison *deftly* handles the issue of . . .

> The second stanza *subtly* introduces the theme of . . .

These words effectively convey critical approval. But you need to be careful in using them, because they can introduce meanings you may not intend. The first example above, for instance, implies that Dickens took special care not to represent Chancery in a particular way, which is something we can never know (we cannot know what was going on in Dickens's head). Many literary theories deny the possibility of talking about intention; so you should be careful – especially if your essay assumes one of these theories – not to let your language make claims that you do not intend. The third of the examples above suggests that the poem is being subtle (whereas in fact it is the author – though again, this is arguably a matter of unknowable intention); use of such personification involves a minor lapse in logic which you should be aware of, even if you decide that the final effect is worth it.

4.7 TECHNICALITY

Literary critics vary in how technical they think literary criticism should be. Running through the history of literary criticism is a series of debates over the connection (or contrast) between literature and philosophy, and between the aesthetic imagination and science. The result is a range of different genres of literary criticism and literary theory, to some extent distinguished by register.

One of the important differences between the registers involves the use of TECHNICAL TERMS. The term 'donor', for example, is specific to a genre which we might call 'writing about narrative in a tradition following Vladimir Propp'; and the term 'the Imaginary' is specific to the genre 'recent psychoanalytically-influenced criticism'. Sometimes the same term means different things in different genres – for example 'discourse' has one meaning in the genre of 'post-structuralist literary theory' but a different meaning in the genre of 'stylistics'. Then again, there are other genres which try to avoid using any technical terms at all, in the belief that literary studies should be accessible to all without special training in a professional vocabulary.

As you will certainly need to use technical terms at some point in your writing, you inevitably have to face the two main problems they present. The first is that of ensuring that your reader knows which words are the technical terms. You can solve this problem by putting such terms in inverted commas when you first introduce them. The second, more difficult problem is that of ensuring that your reader understands what your technical terms mean. To solve this you have to make it clear what genre of writing you are working in (which is partly a matter of the overall register you establish); the technical terms will then be understood according to the conventions of that genre. Sometimes, despite this strategy, you will need to use a term which is not part of the conventional fabric of discourse in which you are working. In this case you should offer a GLOSS (i.e. an explanation or paraphrase), as in the following example (the gloss is italicised):

> In these lines of the poem, the 'structural parallelism', *or equivalence of grammatical structure between the two phrases*, makes us consider the two phrases synonymous.

As long as they do not become too obtrusive, such glosses serve to embed technical terms effectively even within a register which is in other respects informal, or even impressionistic. When you first introduce a technical term which needs explanation, either explain it immediately or indicate that you will explain it shortly. Your reader will then know that you are not presuming that she or he knows what the term means. Nevertheless, one problem with using glosses is that you need to decide which terms to gloss; some terms will have conventional meanings in the genre you are writing in, while other terms – like 'synonymous' in the above quotation – will be common in non-technical discourse. You can get help with deciding whether to explain a term by consulting a dictionary of critical terms, to see which terms other people – the dictionary's editor, for example – have decided merit explanation.

In general, technical description is only appropriate if it illustrates a point in your argument, as can be seen from problems in the following excerpt:

> The sonnet structure is appropriate to the subject. The rhyme scheme of the sonnet is not recognizable as being either a Shakespearean or Petrarchan sonnet; the scheme is ababababcccdcd. However, this is with half-rhymes which sometimes only vaguely go together, for example 'shine' and 'join'. This type of

uncomfortable rhyming creates the impression of the author having difficulty weaving his, or her, emotions.

One problem here is that 'shine' and 'join' were much closer to rhyming when this eighteenth-century poem was written than they are now. Far more important, though, is the problem that there is no reason to assume that half-rhymes signify difficulty in organising emotions, or that a formally ambiguous sonnet is particularly 'appropriate' to an elegy. Without the case for these assumptions being established, the formal description merely signals that the writer knows roughly what a sonnet is.

4.8 DISTANCING YOURSELF FROM OTHER PEOPLE'S TERMS

When introduced for the first time, technical terms can be helpfully identified by having inverted commas round them. This shows that they are words you are mentioning, or borrowing from another type of discourse, rather than words which you are using 'in your own voice'. Another, contrasting function served by inverted commas (besides direct quotation, which is discussed below, Chapter 5, pp. 105–7) is that of distancing you from an expression. Sometimes this is desirable because the expression seems awkward or inadequate; sometimes it signals that the expression does not fit in with the rest of the style (e.g. because of its register).

Such inverted commas are often called SCARE QUOTES, and are used especially in philosophically-inspired criticism which is sceptical about the customary senses we give to words. The scare quotes sound the alarm, and so alert readers to the idea that something is deficient or inappropriate about the word being used.

Take care, however. While it is valuable to show your awareness of complexities in the words through which we conceptualise, scare quotes may not be the best way of doing so. In some cases, consulting a thesaurus will offer an alternative. In other cases, explicit discussion of the difficulties presented by the expression is more helpful, if this does not distract too much from the progression of your argument. Remember that scare quotes themselves are simply disclaimers ('this isn't my word, so don't blame me for its implications'); they do not solve – or even identify – the problems that the word presents. At worst, they merely signal a reluctance or inability to grapple with those problems.

Philosophically, it could be argued in any case that most or all words present analogous difficulties, and need to be put in scare quotes ('the

"topic" of this "essay" is the "issue" of the "author's" "intentions" ',
etc.). So if you start using scare quotes, it may be the words you do not
put them round which become the problem.

4.9 AGENCY AND PASSIVES

It is possible to arrange a sentence in different ways, to emphasise different
aspects of the action it describes. We can formulate an ACTIVE sentence,
for example, where the subject of the verb (italicised below) is the actor:

> *Jane Austen* transforms the evolution of the novel.

Or we can describe the same action using a PASSIVE sentence, in which
the subject of the sentence (italicised below) is acted upon (rather than
acting).

> *The evolution of the novel* is transformed by Jane Austen.

Passives are characteristic of the register of scientific papers, as can be seen
in the scientific preference for passive 'Sodium chloride was added to the
solution', rather than active 'I added sodium chloride to the solution'.

One aspect of scientific style, however, is that in a passive sentence the
person who acts is often not mentioned at all, to symbolise the scientific
ideal that the procedures should be objective and repeatable, independent
of the agent who carries them out. The missing actor is usually assumed
to be the writer. In a literary essay, however, you should be cautious
about leaving out the actor in a passive sentence. In the following passive
sentence the writer does not tell us who did the associating (newspapers?
literary critics? the general public? everyone?):

> The Yellow Book and the Decadents were always associated with
> Oscar Wilde.

Notice, too, that your choice between active or passive has the effect
of enabling you to move the 'actor' and the 'acted upon' around in the
sentence, most often either to the beginning or to the end (as in the 'Jane
Austen' example above). These two positions of special prominence have
different functions, and contribute to the ordering of given and new
information in your writing (we have seen above how presupposition also
contributes to the patterning of given and new, Chapter 3, p. 65). The
beginning of a sentence generally introduces what it is 'about', often an
item of given information (i.e. something which has already been
mentioned or has been directly implied). The end, by contrast, gives focus

or emphasis to new information, and is generally the most appropriate position for the 'point' of what you are saying.

As you write, the process of ordering elements in this way usually happens spontaneously – as it does routinely in conversation. But if a passage you have written seems confused, yet you think it says basically what you want it to say, it can be worth moving elements by changing around active and passive constructions (or experimenting with cleft and pseudo-cleft constructions, which are described above, Chapter 3, p. 64). As you make such changes, you will notice subtly changing effects created by bringing different parts of what you have written into emphasised or FOCUS positions.

4.10   USE OF RHETORICAL QUESTIONS

A rhetorical question is a question you ask in order to create an effect; you do not expect an answer and instead offer one yourself. Rhetorical questions can be a good way of signalling the DIALOGIC nature of your writing (i.e. that it is 'like a dialogue'): they show that you are engaging with your reader, by anticipating her or his responses and questions as you go along.

But rhetorical questions can be over-used, especially where answers to the questions do not follow immediately. Consider these two rhetorical questions, from an essay on *Othello*:

> Does this tell us about Shakespeare? Is he guilty of racial discrimination?

If the essay now abandons these questions and introduces another topic, then the questions have not engaged directly with the reader but have suspended debate, after having introduced, tantalisingly, an area for speculation. In this case, note that the essay goes on,

> The aim is not to apportion blame but to uncover the origins of racial stereotyping and how they have permeated English Literature.

The general issue of 'racial discrimination' is picked up here, in the idea of 'racial stereotyping'; but the specific issue of Shakespeare's guilt is not – it has been raised but not dealt with. Rhetorical questions work, then, when they are answered in what follows, and so long as they are not over-used.

4.11   STYLISTIC INFECTION

In some essays, the style of the language in which the essay is written 'catches' characteristics of the material the essay is about. The result is poetic texts about poems; ironic essays about ironic texts; satirical texts about satire, etc. Often this effect on essay style comes from enthusiasm on the part of the essay-writer for the style of the passage being discussed. But one consequence of such stylistic infection is that it reduces the difference between the text being written about and the essay, and dissolves the boundary (and difference of purpose) between the two. There are things about irony which it may not be possible to say ironically; so an ironic essay on irony will fail to address such issues. In examinations this can be a particular problem, in that it is likely such writing will not answer the prescribed question very closely. Note, too, that if you write ironically you may seem to be satirising the question, or the process of analytical writing about literature more generally.

4.12   YOURSELF AND YOUR READER

When referring to yourself as the writer, it is possible to use a range of forms: 'I', 'we', 'one', 'the present author', etc. Traditionally, there are restrictions on using 'I': some teachers forbid it, as an example of inelegant intrusion by the author (though nowadays it is generally thought permissible to use 'I' occasionally, to emphasise a point which you wish to show is personal rather than general). The guiding principle must be that the overall value or interest of the essay lies in how its combination of observation and argument leads towards more general statements, and so away from the particularity of autobiography and personal impression. In this respect, too much use of 'I' (especially, 'I think', 'I noticed', 'I much prefer', etc.) prevents the essay from attaining that level of generalisation.

It is possible to get round the need to refer to yourself by using the following devices, which can be varied in order to avoid any over-formulaic effect:

 - *Adverbs and adverbial expressions* Instead of 'I think it is likely that . . .' use 'Arguably . . .' (but bear in mind what we have said about 'arguably' above, Chapter 3, p. 68).
 - *Passives* Rewrite 'I argue below that . . .' as 'it is argued below that . . .'
 - *Personification of your essay itself as an agent* Rewrite 'in this essay I explain how . . .' as 'this essay explains how . . .'

'One' and 'we' as ways of referring to yourself should be avoided because they now seem ARCHAIC (old-fashioned), and in most cases pompous in an unpublished essay, especially if embedded in a more colloquial register. The authorial 'we' ('we will argue below') should similarly be avoided. This recommendation to avoid 'one' and 'we' has a justification besides traditional reservations about personal intrusion. Both 'one' and 'we' produce the effect of generalised response: 'one' combines the personal dimension of 'I' with the general characteristic of 'anyone' (i.e. the writer serves as a norm or representative of everyone else); and 'we' (at least in its inclusive use as readers, 'we feel in this passage', rather than as authorial 'we, the author') suggests generalised reader-reaction. Clearly it is possible to use 'a reader', or 'the reader' to replace 'we' in this sense, with an analogous implication of common, general response. Alternatively, however, you may want to emphasise the point that actual readers are unlikely to respond all in the same way, especially readers differing in gender, class, age, ethnicity or some other aspect of social identity. So you may want to modify such formulations along the lines, 'a reader is likely to feel at this point' or 'many readers may respond by . . .', or – possibly better – by tackling the issue of heterogeneous reader-responses more directly.

The precise degree to which you decide to use techniques for avoiding 'I' and 'we' will depend on the overall register you are trying to produce. But you should certainly avoid obvious personal intrusions, such as the two following:

> *The confession* 'Sorry, I had no time to complete this essay, so I have made some basic points that I would have brought out and discussed.'
>
> *The embedded 'letter'* (a direct address to the reader, often with apology or denunciation of the course): 'Isn't there a problem with the way you have formulated this question? I should have thought that . . .'

So much, then, for 'I'. But what about 'you'? In this book you will probably have noticed that we use 'you' quite often. Yet second-person pronouns are not generally accepted in academic writing, a characteristic of the idiom linked to the idea of criticism having less a given, particular reader than of an unspecified general readership. While this view of a readership is often deeply at odds with the actual circumstances of essay-writing in literature courses, it remains a conventional feature of academic style; and your writing will produce very marked effects if you deviate from the conventions it has produced. Ways round using 'you' overlap with the ways of avoiding 'I' and 'we' outlined above. Replace,

for example, 'in this essay I will tell you' with 'this essay explains how
. . .', and 'you might see this phrase as meaning . . .' with something
like 'this phrase may be interpreted as meaning . . .'

4.13 UNBIASED AND GENDER-FREE LANGUAGE

If this book had been written twenty years ago it would have been
unlikely to contain any discussion of bias in the language of academic
work. Because of changes in society in general, and in the student and
academic population in particular, bias has become a major issue in
academic writing (reflected for example in current arguments over
'political correctness'). 'Biased language' is language which favours one
group of the population at the expense of another; the group not favoured
is then said to be marginalised or derogated. There are two basic
mechanisms by which bias works: choice of pronouns (specifically in the
case of gender bias), and choice of names for people.

Consider this sentence:

The reader will find his expectations satisfied.

The writer of this sentence doesn't know whether the reader is male or
female, but has chosen to use 'his' as a GENERIC to mean 'male or
female', overriding the normal use of 'his' as a gender-specific pronoun
meaning 'male'. While this used to be common practice, it is now widely
considered sexist: such usage represents the masculine as the norm, and so
marginalises women. In the case of the link between 'reader . . . he', the
'male as norm' terminology creates the impression that educated discussion
of literature takes place only among men (even though literary study was
established in Britain in the nineteenth century as a subject largely for
women, and now has a significant majority of women involved in it).
Such usage also reinforces the common but mistaken idea that authors are
normally men rather than women (an idea which is probably only true of
the canon of writers selected for study – generally by male critics – not of
writing as a whole).

There are various alternatives to traditional, 'generic' usage. Both male
and female pronouns can be used:

The reader will find his or her expectations satisfied.

But there is no particular reason to put 'his' first, so you could also write:

The reader will find her or his expectations satisfied.

Or you can rewrite the sentence so that the plural pronoun is used:

> Readers will find their expectations satisfied.

Or you can use 's/he' and 'her/his' to replace 'he and/or she'. Or you can use 'she' *as a generic*, directly challenging the older use of 'he':

> The reader will find her expectations satisfied.

Finally, some writers alternate 'he' and 'she' (for example, in Open University coursebooks, alternative paragraphs have 'he' or 'she'; and in Sperber and Wilson's linguistic work, *Relevance Theory*, the speaker is always referred to as 'she' – 's' for 'speaker' – and the hearer as 'he' – 'h' for 'hearer'). Any of these methods is satisfactory; the important thing is to be consistent.

The second major way of expressing bias is in the use of names for groups of people. The false generic 'Man/mankind' should be replaced by 'people', 'humankind', ' etc.; and further bias against women is expressed by referring to adult women as 'girls'. Similarly, you should avoid terms such as 'poetess', 'actress', 'lady novelist', etc., which are all asymmetrical with the male–counterpart term ('poet', 'actor', etc.). Lists of names of authors should not be differentiated according to gender, by using first names for female writers but only family names for male writers (as in 'Shakespeare, Milton, Jane Austen, Hardy'). Be consistent in whatever listing convention you choose.

While bias against women is perhaps the most thorough form of bias in language, it is important to recognise and try to remove bias against other marginalised groups. In general, groups of people must be allowed to choose their own names: no group chooses to call itself 'Red Indians' or 'Negroes', so you should avoid these terms; 'coloured' is generally considered unacceptable by people to whom the term is applied; etc. Naming groups of people is an extremely complex issue, which is dependent on the political orientations of the people involved and on rapid changes in nuance and connotation. But you cannot simply opt out of the issue altogether, no matter who you are: whatever choice you make in this area will have a meaning and give a signal.

Making yourself aware of bias and adopting alternative usages should prevent the tacit presumption by your reader of the white male as a norm. It also signals in passing your awareness of issues of gender, race and other questions of social distinction which arise in literary study; this awareness should then extend into your choice of particular texts and authors to study, and into the comments and analysis of images of gender, sexuality and difference you develop.

4.14 SUMMARY, SUGGESTIONS AND EXERCISES

Summary In this chapter, we have suggested that literary essays have a characteristic style or voice which is different from the way you talk or might narrate a story or write a letter. In describing the various features of this academic essay-writing register, we have stressed that the style you adopt not only places your essay in an established, conventional idiom, but also creates a clear impression of you and your attitudes towards your subject matter, as well as defining a specific relationship with your reader. Adopting an inappropriate style can accordingly damage your credibility as a writer, and undermine the force of the points your essay makes. Conversely, developing your skill with the nuances of essay-writing style can enhance the effect of the points you make, and enable you to steer comfortably through complexities of the arguments you present.

Specific suggestions:

* ⋆ Develop a register for your academic writing which avoids characteristics of speech but which you can still comfortably read aloud (see pp. 73–4).
* ⋆ Use a mixture of short sentences and longer, more complex sentences (see pp. 76–7).
* ⋆ Use the same register throughout an essay (see pp. 77–8).
* ⋆ Avoid being condescending to your reader or about the text you are discussing (see pp. 78–9).
* ⋆ Use technical terms only when you are going to say something with them which you couldn't say without them (see pp. 81–2).
* ⋆ Explain technical terms, particularly if your writing is not rooted in a specific theoretical or critical tradition; if the terms you are using seem difficult to explain, avoid them if you can, or at least explain the difficulty (see p. 81).
* ⋆ Ask rhetorical questions only when you are going to give an answer to them (see p. 84).
* ⋆ Don't copy the style of a literary text you are writing about (see p. 85).
* ⋆ Don't refer to yourself as 'one' or 'we'; use 'I' only when you want to introduce a special, personal note (see p. 86).
* ⋆ Don't address the reader directly; avoid 'you' (see pp. 86–7).
* ⋆ Don't use biased language; in particular, don't use 'he' to mean both men and women (see pp. 87–8).

Exercises

(1) This chapter is not written in a standard academic register (such as you might use in an essay). Take the paragraph on p. 73 beginning 'On the whole . . .', underline all parts of it which might be considered not to belong to standard academic register and explain why, and rewrite the paragraph in academic register. When you do this, bear in mind the need to avoid bias in the use of pronouns (section 4.13).

(2) Rewrite the extract on p. 77 beginning 'Since Etherege . . .', so that it consists of several short sentences.

(3) Rewrite the extract on p. 78 beginning 'Moore states . . .', so that its register is consistent (and neither too high nor too low for academic writing).

(4) The following passage contains some inconsistencies in terms of the register it adopts. Using our discussion in this chapter, edit it so that it conforms more to what you now understand to be conventions of an appropriate literary-critical style. (Try to alter the sense of the passage as little as possible in your revisions.)

> There is dichotomy in the defiance of moral law in Marlowe's
> *Edward II.* For at the play's inception Edward is berated by
> Mortimer and the other earls for his base acts with Gaveston; and in
> defiance of well-defined laws of divine right and birthright
> Mortimer attempts to depose a crowned king. Both acts are morally
> wrong – Edward should not have abused his divine right and
> curried favour by dishing out peerages. Conversely Mortimer should
> not have invoked the earls to revolt against the king. So at the nub
> of Marlowe's play is the morality of deposition and the morality of a
> married king shunning his wife in favour of a homosexual lover.

4.15   YOUR OWN NOTES ON THIS CHAPTER

1

2

3

4

5

Writing your essay or dissertation

This chapter looks at how you compose the sentences and paragraphs which make up your essay or dissertation. In particular, we consider two especially important parts of your work: the beginning and the end. The beginning has to create interest and tell the reader what to expect, while the end will form a disproportionate part of the reader's final impression of your essay (in fact, many readers will read the end first, to find out what conclusions you draw). Later sections of the chapter explain how you divide your essay into paragraphs and signal the relationship between them. We end by looking at how you embed other people's words into your own writing, in the form of paraphrase and quotation.

5.1 THE FIRST PARAGRAPH

The first paragraph of your essay tells your reader what your essay will be about: what the main focus is and what question(s) you are going to answer. But your first paragraph is also your opportunity to start actively working on those questions. This is true even if the question has been prescribed by someone else (perhaps in an examination); in such cases, you reformulate the question in your first paragraph to demonstrate that you have understood it and can develop arguments from it.

Here is an example of a set question:

> Explain fully the significance of the title of 'The Captain's Doll'.

And this is the beginning of an essay which answers it:

The significance of the title of 'The Captain's Doll' is its use as a central symbol or motif which is the organizing principle for the whole story. Though the doll motif can be applied to several different characters, its central meaning is a representation of that which Lawrence dislikes in relationships between men and women.

The essay begins by stating its main point: that the title focuses attention on a multifunctional symbol within the story. But to do this, the writer simply repeats the wording of the question. Instead she or he could have used material from the question to begin the essay with a generalisation (see above, Chapter 3, p. 66), like this:

> Titles often serve the purpose of focusing attention on a central symbol; and this is certainly true of 'The Captain's Doll'. Though the doll motif . . .

Just repeating the question tells your examiner nothing about what you know, and takes up time and space. Reworking the question into a related generalisation, on the other hand, shows that you understand something of the complexities it contains. Similarly, as you rework the question into your first sentence you can begin to show that key terms in the question are problematic or vague, or you can suggest what kind of evidence you will draw on to discuss the question.

As well as introducing the content of your essay, your first paragraph should also explain its organisation. But don't overdo this by being too overt, as in this opening to an essay (by a non-native speaker) titled 'Lyrical and Epical Genres in Middle English Poetry':

> I shall begin discussing lyrical and epical genres in Middle English poetry with the explanation of both these terms. But before they will be explained it is necessary to consider the term genre. Quoting Burrow . . .

While this beginning is effective in showing organisation, it delays getting into the argument, and could be rewritten in the following way, which both demonstrates organisation less clumsily and gets immediately to the point:

> Since the terms 'lyrical' and 'epic' present special difficulties when used of Middle English works, it is useful to introduce discussion of works of the period with a brief analysis of these two terms. And since the larger concept of 'genre', within which they play a part, is also problematic, my discussion of the two terms will be prefaced by a more general discussion of 'genre'. Interestingly, Burrow's suggestion is that . . .

In its first few lines, the rewritten passage now offers *reasons* for organising the essay in the way that has been chosen, and so connects the answer more directly with the question.

Slightly different problems arise in our next example, though again they are related to the relationship between the various topics being introduced:

> The 'Sonnet on the Death of Mr Richard West' contains many half-rhymes and can be split into two groups, the octave and the sestet. The sonnet is an emotional elegy, and the tone is mournful. The author addresses the reader directly.

In this passage three topics are introduced: the sonnet's form, its tone and its mode of address. But no link is suggested between them, and it is not yet clear what the point of the essay is. We could accordingly rewrite this opening as:

> In the 'Sonnet on the Death of Mr Richard West', formal qualities of the sonnet (such as its rhyme scheme, division between octave and sestet and mode of address) are moulded to suit the mournful tone of an emotional elegy.

In this revised version the individual observations are collected together under a common denominator (labelled 'formal qualities') and are linked to the claimed mood of the poem. Instead of just being presented with a list of topics, we now know the relationship between the topics.

A helpful first paragraph, then, offers your reader a 'menu' of what will follow, while at the same time already beginning on the argument of the essay. But you need to remember that the menu should not be too large (some essays become very front-heavy with preliminaries); and you should ensure that items you have placed on the menu are actually served up to the reader later. Sometimes, the subject areas outlined are impossibly large, given the essay's prescribed length. It is a good test of an opening sentence (or paragraph) to read it aloud, list the topics you think it tells a reader to expect in the essay, and make sure that those topics coincide with your planned contents.

Organising your essay in advance changes the process of writing a first paragraph. Advance planning makes it possible to write the essay in sections and put the sections together only at the end – with the result that you do not have to write the sections in the order in which they will finally appear. You can write your first paragraph when you have finished the rest of the essay; and at that point, you will definitely be able to promise what the essay will cover – because you will have already written it.

5.2 THE LAST PARAGRAPH

Your reader will pay particular attention to your last paragraph and last sentence, largely because the last section has to bring to a suitable conclusion the various different arguments you have made. 'A suitable conclusion' does not mean just repeating your opening sentence. If you begin like this:

> In this essay, I will argue that Henry James's representations and frequent treatment of women through metaphors as art objects are deeply problematic.

You should *not* end your essay by simply recapitulating:

> In the foregoing pages, I have shown how Henry James's representations and frequent treatment of women through metaphors as art objects are deeply problematic.

Such repetition is simply a reminder, not a conclusion. In a long dissertation it might be justified as a way of helping your reader remember your starting point; in a short essay, however, it is redundant and simply shows that you don't know how to finish.

What then would be a 'suitable conclusion'? This depends on the aims of the essay, but it might include:

- a judgement about which of the competing arguments you have considered in your essay is correct or most persuasive;
- an evaluation or assessment of the qualities of a work or writer, based on arguments presented in the essay;
- an indication of what consequences follow from what you have shown in your essay.

If you want to suggest consequences or implications, try ending by answering these questions:

(a) Have you discovered any methods which can now be used to investigate another text or author?

(b) Does your argument suggest that we should look again at some other area, which we might now view differently?

(c) Can you extend what you have said to other works by the same author, by other authors, or to other works of the same period?

(d) Can you make any important general observations, using your whole essay as an illustration or case study?

Each of the questions above is worth exploring, especially because final paragraphs and sentences often fall into one of a number of largely unsatisfactory idioms, each with its own way of dealing with ending less as an opportunity than as an escape. We indicate some of the idioms below.

The 'farewell speech'

Avoid the sort of ending used in this essay on 'Genres of the Old English Poetry':

> And in this way we have come to the end of our characterisation of the main genres of the oldest vernacular poetry in Western Europe; poetry which achieved so great variety over the 8th, 9th, and 10th centuries.

The phrase 'come to the end of our' suggests a pleasant, shared experience or excursion; and the expression 'oldest vernacular poetry in Western Europe' calls to mind less the language of analysis or scholarship than that of advertising or publicity (where things are valued because they are the best, the oldest, etc.). These features of the style, coupled with the exclamatory force of 'so' ('so great variety') give an overall effect that the conclusion is a promotional, or uncritically praising, piece of writing, rather than an academic study. Both the intentions and the style of this final sentence are inappropriate.

Indecisiveness disguised as fairness

Your essay is an argument, and you should present different sides of that argument. It is this argument which your first paragraph promises and to which your last paragraph offers a conclusion. But your conclusion can properly come to a decision on one side, and need not remain balanced (so avoid: 'both sides have their virtues and it is difficult to decide between them'). It is perfectly acceptable to draw conclusions of your own, based on the arguments and evidence you have presented. The challenge is to show that you have answered the question but have got there by fair consideration of all positions.

Falling over backwards

Consider this final sentence from an essay on the element of satire in two Restoration dramatists:

> Both playwrights succeed in mixing description with analysis which is conveyed in entertaining prose.

Here the problem lies in the generality of the terms 'description' and 'analysis', as well as in the anti-climactic phrase 'entertaining prose' as the final words of the piece. 'Entertaining' is too unspecific a notion, as though you had slipped backwards in the argument after reaching more sophisticated peaks of describing the details of satire. The point of an ending is for the conclusion to *look* backwards, not to carry the argument backwards.

The higher authority

When you write an essay you have both the opportunity *and* the responsibility to state your own views in your own words. It is often tempting to think that some critic you have read can summarise your viewpoint better than you yourself can, and so to end your essay with a quotation from someone else. We talk later in this chapter about the use of other people's words, making the point that one problem with other people's words is that they usually make more sense where they come from than where you put them in your essay. Because your conclusion is so important, you can't risk the slightly different emphases and directions which someone else's words are likely to carry. Because your essay is not identical with theirs, there is little chance that someone else's words will be exactly right as a conclusion to your argument.

The disconnected personal opinion

Concluding with your own words, however, requires caution, particularly in the handling of personal response. Despite the instruction often given by teachers to emphasise personal involvement towards the end of an essay, you should avoid the sort of over-personalised ending found in this essay:

> After reading the first paragraph, I didn't expect such an exciting story, but gradually I got more and more involved in the narrative and finally overwhelmed by this splendid spectacle, which I could vividly visualise.

This sudden introduction of personal involvement into an essay which was otherwise a dispassionate description is disruptive, and sounds as though the writer really wanted to write much more personally (so indicating a kind of dissatisfaction with the essay as it stands).

5.3   DIVIDING YOUR ESSAY INTO SECTIONS AND PARAGRAPHS

Having considered its two most prominent sections – the beginning and the end – we turn now to the structure of the rest – the 'body' – of the essay. Like a human body, the body of your essay is made up of parts: in this case paragraphs and perhaps numbered or titled sections and subsections. You should gather all your ideas on the same general point into the same section of the essay, so that the essay seems to move forward consistently rather than jump around; you can test whether the essay does have this sort of organisation by working out an appropriate title for each section and paragraph (even though in the final version of the essay your paragraphs at least will lose their titles).

Your outline (see above, Chapter 1, pp. 22–4 and Chapter 3, pp. 59–61) will indicate what needs to go into each part of your essay, and enables you to write the different parts in any order you wish. Each topic in the sequence of topics contained in your outline can be translated into a section of your essay. In a short essay the sections will be paragraphs; in a long essay you can combine the paragraphs into titled and or numbered sections and sub-sections. In making these organisational decisions, however, you need to ensure that you do not put in *too many* markers of structure, which can make the essay seem to be all scaffolding with no building inside. Management of your essay should not overwhelm its content.

One major reason for breaking your essay into parts is to signal how each part relates to the whole. Accordingly, as you convert your plan into a series of sections or paragraph topics, you should think carefully about the logical or rhetorical relationship between them: e.g. cause and effect; particularisation and specification; illustration (if so, of what exactly?). Each paragraph should begin with a sentence which relates what comes next to the last point you have made and to the structure of the essay as a whole. This does not need to be done explicitly (e.g. through devices such as 'in the last paragraph, I have argued . . .'), but can be achieved by phrases like 'this x', or 'the idea that x' (where x is a term or phrase used in the previous paragraph).

If you do use sub-sections you can number them (1, 1.1, 1.2, etc.) or give them short titles which indicate what they contain. Avoid formal labels, such as 'Introduction' and 'Conclusion', which are redundant; instead you might say something along the lines of 'Introduction: symbolism as an issue in "The Captain's Doll" '. A useful test of how effective your section headings are is that it should be possible to string them together into a paraphrase of what the essay says.

Your reader knows what is in a section because it has a title. A paragraph, on the other hand, has its main point or direction indicated in the opening sentence, which is sometimes called a TOPIC SENTENCE. (Sometimes the closing sentence performs a similar role.) It can be useful practice to read through the first sentences of paragraphs which make up a published essay, to see how much work – of summary and of signposting – is being done by these 'topic sentences'. Paragraphs do not function identically in all languages and cultures, however. So paragraphing may present some bilingual writers working in a second language with greater difficulties than writers whose experience is confined to the language and culture in which they are writing.

Typically in English a paragraph is unified by the fact that it brings together material around a single point or topic indicated in the first sentence. One way of doing this is to structure your paragraph as:

First sentence (topic sentence), makes the main claim of the paragraph (and tries also to link the paragraph with what came before)

+ *subsequent sentences*: justify or illustrate the claim;
+ *final sentence*: sums up the paragraph (and perhaps tries also to link the paragraph with what will come next).

This basic pattern is illustrated by the following, complete four-sentence paragraph (here split into parts and with sentence numbers added).

Topic sentence (which makes the main claim of the paragraph):
(1) In Chapter 2 Fitzgerald introduces one of the most important patterns of the novel: the 'waste land motif'.

Subsequent sentences (which justify or illustrate the claim):
(2) Nothing in the book emphasises the corruption of the American dream more than this image of 'the valley of ashes'.
(3) In 1922 T.S. Eliot published his highly influential poem, 'The Waste Land', in which he described Western civilisation in terms of decay and desperation.

Final sentence (which sums up the paragraph):
(4) In *The Great Gatsby* Fitzgerald picks up the theme: the valley of ashes is the general locale, all the characters of the story have to pass through it.

Sentence (1) introduces the topic of the paragraph: the functioning of the 'waste land motif' in the organisation of *The Great Gatsby*. Sentence (2) then offers a meaning for the motif: a critique of the corruption of the American dream. Sentence (3) opens with an apparent change of topic, but implicitly connects the new topic with the already established topic of the paragraph in a thematic parallel – to be found in T.S. Eliot's concern with 'decay and desperation' – which also provides a source for the name of the motif, the 'waste land motif'. Finally, in sentence (4) the parallel between Eliot and Fitzgerald is drawn explicitly, and the way the motif works in the novel is explained, so completing a miniature demonstration of what was promised in the paragraph's opening, topic sentence.

A short essay covering four A4 pages (about 1,200 words) might well be divided into about eight paragraphs. Too few paragraphs can make the essay difficult to follow, both visually and conceptually, and suggests that it may not have an underlying argument structure at all. If the paragraphs are consistently very short, on the other hand (e.g. just one or two sentences), then the subdivisions being made become too complicated for a more general, structural image of the essay to be deduced, which defeats the point of having paragraphs at all. In general terms, a paragraph should have several sentences, and might cover about half a page of A4 (about 100 to 150 words).

5.4   SIGNPOSTING AND CONNECTIVES

It is not only headings and topic sentences at the beginning of paragraphs which signal the directions in which an essay is progressing, however. Most sentences in written prose are explicitly linked with the sentence which precedes them, producing an overall effect of COHESION. Consider this brief passage, from an essay by a non-native speaker (numbers have been added to identify sentences):

> [1] One of the functions of a literary work is to pass on some crucial truths or information, give some didactic indications, or convince the reader of some general laws. [2] The dream vision convention was employed by the Middle English writers for such reasons; [3] and it enjoyed great popularity. [4] Discovering this literary phenomenon, we should realise that the contemporary reader of Middle English lived in a different social and cultural reality from ours. [5] So the dream vision must have had a tremendous impact on his perception of the world.

Notice that this paragraph is not only held together by the sort of unity, or development of ideas, that we described in the *Great Gatsby* example above. We can also identify a series of formal markers of connection between the respective sentences. Sentence (2) is connected to (1), for instance, by the phrase 'for such reasons', which refers back to the reasons listed in (1), as well as by the fact that the 'dream vision convention' is recognisable as an aspect of 'a literary work' referred to in (1). Sentence (3) is linked to (2) by the additive connective 'and', as well as by the fact that 'it' refers back to 'dream vision convention'. Sentence (4) is connected with (3) by the word 'this', which again refers to 'dream vision convention', as well as by the repetition of 'Middle English'. Sentence (5) connects with (4) because of a number of features: the repetition of 'dream vision'; the logical connection indicated by 'so'; the connection in meaning between 'world' and the phrase 'social and cultural reality'; and by the fact that 'his' refers back to the 'contemporary reader'.

What is significant about formal markers of this kind is that they achieve two related effects in academic writing (as in discourse more generally). Firstly, they bind a piece of writing together as a single entity, giving it a connectedness that makes it read as a whole rather than as a string of separate jottings. Secondly, many of the markers signal specific – often logical – relationships between one sentence and another (as 'so' does in the passage above); such markers control the progression of your writing from idea to idea. For this reason it is important in essay-writing to learn how to handle markers of cohesion, and to sensitise yourself to the underlying relations of meaning they signal.

The formal markers of connectedness described above indicate in general that one statement is about to be amplified, supported or qualified by, or alternatively contrasted with, the next statement. There are a range of signals which can be used in this way. Each indicates quite specifically how a following statement will build on the preceding one, and we list some of them in the grid on the following pages. Read along the top of the grid to see *kinds of transition*, and down the left-hand side for a *list of common connective expressions*.

It is a good test of an essay's cohesion to work through a draft underlining all its cohesive devices, perhaps using the list we provide here. Cohesive markers are not always necessary, but where you find sentences without evident markers, it may be useful to inspect them closely to be certain that the relationship with the preceding sentence is sufficiently clear.

Do not think, though, that simply because you have inserted cohesive devices the logical or rhetorical relationships of your essay are therefore adequately constructed. It is possible to use cohesive markers which are incompatible with the sentences they are supposed to link; the resulting effect is one of a cohesive text which remains incoherent. Consider in this light the following example:

	consequence	likeness	contrast	amplification	example	particularisation	concession	insistence	sequence	restatement	recapitulation	time or place
above												✓
accordingly	✓											
afterwards												✓
again				✓								
all in all											✓	
also				✓								
altogether											✓	
analogously		✓										
and				✓								
as a result	✓											
at the same time												✓
below												✓
but			✓									
correspondingly		✓										
earlier												✓
elsewhere												✓
especially						✓						
finally									✓			
first									✓			
for example					✓							
for instance					✓							
formerly												✓
further			✓									
further on												✓
furthermore			✓									
granted that							✓					
hence	✓											
here												✓
hitherto												✓
however			✓									
in addition				✓								

	consequence	likeness	contrast	amplification	example	particularisation	concession	insistence	sequence	restatement	recapitulation	time or place
in conclusion											✓	
in fact								✓				
in other words										✓		
in particular						✓						
in simpler terms										✓		
indeed								✓				
it is true that							✓					
later												✓
moreover				✓								
nevertheless			✓									
next									✓			
of course							✓					
on the contrary			✓									
on the other hand			✓									
second									✓			
similarly		✓										
simultaneously												✓
so far												✓
subsequently												✓
that is										✓		
that is to say										✓		
then	✓											
there												✓
therefore	✓											
this time												✓
thus	✓											
to put the point another way										✓		
to summarise											✓	
too				✓								
until now												✓
yet			✓									

103

It is unlikely that Shakespeare or the majority of writers in construction of their work imagined the twentieth-century reader or considered the possibility that the reader would be of another race or colour than his own (the exception to this assumption can be found in later twentieth-century writers). However, Shakespeare wrote 'Othello'.

Notice here the slight oddity of 'however'. It is clear that an element of contrast is intended, with a meaning something like 'in writing *Othello*, Shakespeare becomes an exception, and so stands in contrast to other writers'. But the effect of 'however' here does not focus the contrast in quite this way. Rather, 'however' creates a contrast concerning the idea of a writer foreseeing the effect on later audiences – something which pulls the essay in a different direction from one which might create the expectation that *Othello* would be introduced.

Alongside the sorts of connective listed above, other kinds of link can also be useful. Sometimes a DISJUNCT can be used, a word or phrase which tells your reader what your attitude or degree of commitment is towards the material you present. Disjuncts act as ways of indicating your evaluation of someone else's view which you are representing.

hearsay disjuncts:(allegedly, reportedly, etc.)
'Reportedly, Yeats was particularly fond of this poem . . .'
evidential disjuncts:(clearly, obviously, etc.)
'Clearly it would be rash to assume that Shakespeare knew of this earlier version.'

Less common, but sometimes useful, are:

attitudinal disjuncts:(unfortunately, sadly, luckily, etc.)
'Sadly, this was the last novel Hardy was to write'. . .'

Note, however, that attitudinal disjuncts can sometimes have an odd effect on the register of your essay, and are therefore less easily incorporated.

As well as holding your text together, cohesive markers and disjuncts are tools for managing your essay. You need to stand back from what you write and explicitly present it to your reader, commenting directly on its organisation, rather than just on the ideas it contains. By referring to your essay in this way, you can direct your reader to specific parts of it, perhaps for emphasis; and you can comment on and mediate your material. MEDIATION is the process of acting as a go-between, or guide. Mediating devices include phrases like, 'as I have shown above', 'so far I have tried to argue that', 'it may be helpful here to distinguish between', 'in this section', 'in my introductory paragraph', etc. They also include brief summaries of what has gone before, or even direct repetition of key points, though this must be clearly for the benefit of the reader, not just to fill up space.

Over-use of such mediating devices is unwise, especially where they involve direct repetition. But in our experience, this kind of metacommentary in essays at all levels (from 'A' level through to PhD writing) tends to be under-used; readers are left to infer connections and linkages for themselves, and the effectiveness of sections of argument is as a result often significantly reduced. Generally what is needed is far greater signalling of what is going on in an essay, and more explicit management of the material presented.

5.5   USING OTHER PEOPLE'S WORDS (QUOTATION AND PARAPHRASE)

In writing a literary essay, you will almost certainly at some point want to incorporate someone else's words. This is not only because quotation contributes to an appropriate 'literary critical' register (for this dubious reason, quotations are often believed to be 'compulsory in essays'); it is also because your essays are largely *about language* (both the language of the literary texts you are analysing and also the language of critical works about them), so quotation is the main way of presenting essential data.

You can either quote or paraphrase literary texts; and the same is true of critical analyses. The differences between quotation and paraphrase can be seen in the following contrasting examples:

Quotation
'One of the most striking things about detective fiction', Patricia Craig argues in her critical introduction to English detective stories, 'is the ease with which it accommodates all kinds of topical ideologies.'

Paraphrase (or summary)
It is among the most striking features of detective fiction, Patricia Craig points out, that all kinds of topical ideologies are easily accommodated within it.

Mixture of paraphrase and quotation
One of the most striking features of detective fiction, as Patricia Craig points out, is the way in which it 'accommodates all kinds of topical ideologies'.

The most obvious difference between quotation and paraphrase in these examples is the punctuation which separates a quotation from the surrounding material. Notice that the verbs of reporting are shared: 'argues', 'suggests', 'points out', etc., can be used with quotation or with paraphrase (though only in paraphrase is the reporting verb phrase commonly preceded with 'as' and followed by 'that').

A paraphrase usually substantially changes the language of the original, because all that matters is that the idea is conveyed. Normally you would paraphrase rather than quote, because this is a way of rewriting the relevant material in a way which assimilates it into your essay (rather than, as with a quotation, leaving it sticking out because of its different style). But you should use a quotation if the language of the original is itself important.

When you put a quotation in your essay you should do several things with it:

– Identify where the quotation comes from, e.g. the author and work:

as Woolf suggests in *The Common Reader*, '[QUOTE]'.
Early in the essay, Addison refers to this phenomenon as '[QUOTE]'.

– Tell the reader something about the context from which the quotation was taken, to indicate the background against which the quotation is being used. Sometimes this specification of context will be just a phrase, such as:

In the course of a description of Henchard late in the novel, Hardy says, '[QUOTE]'.

– Add a commentary or gloss, clarifying the relevance of the quotation to your argument. Since quoted material can be read in many different ways, you need to ensure that the particular contribution the quotation makes to your argument is made explicit. Take special care with long quoted passages (more than a couple of sentences or more than a few lines of a poem), as a lengthy quotation which is not then followed by detailed analysis and discussion is probably being used (illegitimately) as a way of replacing rather than supporting your argument; you should guide your readers through the significance of what you have selected for their attention.

Literary essays typically follow a simple set of conventions governing the presentation of quotations. In general, short quotations in prose (up to about forty to fifty words) are incorporated in the body of the text, enclosed within single quotation marks. (Some systems recommend double quotation marks; either will be acceptable, as long as you are consistent.) Longer prose quotations are indented as a whole by about half an inch from the left margin of the rest of the text, and should *not* have quotation marks. Quotations in verse should be indented, like long quotations, and laid out as closely as possible to the original.

All quoted material should follow the spelling and punctuation of the source edition. If you omit words from a quotation, indicate the omission by the use of three points (. . .), allowing a blank space on either side. (This is known as an ELLIPSIS.) Any editorial insertions you make within a quotation should be enclosed within square brackets [ ], as in:

> This tendency for the image of war to be *distorted* [my italics] has the effect of . . . encouraging unjustifiable patriotism.

5.6 INDICATING WHERE SOMEONE ELSE'S IDEAS OR WORDS COME FROM

When you use someone else's ideas or words, you need to say where they come from. Traditionally it was the practice to provide a footnote for every reference made in an essay, whether for a quotation or for a paraphrase. In many cases, this loads down an essay with so many notes that it becomes difficult to read. For this reason, the footnote-reference system has been widely displaced by other accepted techniques, such as the system which we now describe, and which we would recommend.

In the Harvard system (often referred to as the 'author–date' style), references to a particular work are made in the form of a parenthesis, giving the author's name, the date of the publication referred to or quoted from and the relevant page number(s). This system works effectively, so long as the work in question can be clearly identified in the booklist or bibliography attached to the essay or dissertation (for details, see below, Chapter 7, pp. 134–5). Where there may be ambiguity, because two works exist that were published by the same author in the same year, the two works can be labelled (a) and (b), as in, Kachru 1982(a) and Kachru 1982(b). Note that for a book written by more than two people your textual reference can normally just give the first of the names, followed by 'et al.' to stand for the other people's names.

Here are some examples of typical references that might occur in the body of your essay:

(Belsey 1980) (= a general reference to the whole work)

(Belsey 1980, 17–21) (= a reference to pp. 17–21 of the work cited)

(*Sir Gawain and the Green Knight* C14) (= a reference to an anonymous work, for which the title rather than an author is given – the date here means fourteenth century.)

Note also that when you cite standard works, such as classical, medieval, scriptural or liturgical works, references should follow the numbered divisions and subdivisions of the text:

Od, III, 28 = *Odyssey*, Book III, line 28.

What we have been outlining here is a simple version of the Harvard system of 'author–date'. Other established systems for presenting references include the Chicago system (the style of the Chicago University Press) and the MHRA system (the style of the Modern Humanities Research Association). In quite a lot of professional academic writing, the various systems are mixed together, despite the fact that most journals seek to adopt a consistent policy and insist on receiving manuscripts which follow a specified system.

In most work you do, it is not especially important which style you use (unless you are required to use a particular system by your teacher or institution). What matters is that you are consistent. Although they are important, you should not let technicalities in presenting references divert you away from the crucial tasks of organising and writing your essay. For 'A' level and undergraduate essays, in most cases, it is sufficient simply to underline titles of books, journals and long poems, and to enclose the titles of articles, short stories, short poems and individual essays in single inverted commas. You should identify sources for quotations, either by the 'author–date' system with a suitable bibliography or by individual footnotes. Bear in mind that presentational matters are for the convenience of your reader, who will want to be able to check easily on the materials you have used.

In writing dissertations and postgraduate theses, on the other hand, it is necessary to explore – and follow – established academic conventions more fully. Among the best places to look for guidance are the relevant manuals themselves (see our Booklist at the end of this book). Differences between the three main systems in use mainly concern punctuation, use of parentheses and the order of elements which must be cited; but while these may seem small discrepancies, it is one part of the process of research to assess at some point the different conventions governing the listing and presentation of sources, and to present work accurately according to whatever set of conventions you are following.

5.7 PLAGIARISM

Whether you quote or paraphrase, it is important that your essay distinguishes clearly between your own words – your own voice, as we have described it above – and those words and ideas you are embedding in your work which originate elsewhere. Failing to make this distinction is called PLAGIARISM and must be avoided. Consider, for example, the following beginning to an essay entitled 'Foregrounding in *King Lear*':

> In its most general interpretation, the word 'style' has a fairly uncontroversial meaning: it refers to the way in which language is used in a given context, by a particular person, for a certain purpose. To make it clear I have to adopt the Swiss linguist Saussure's theory which distinguishes between 'langue' and 'parole'. 'Langue' is the code or system of rules common to speakers of a language like English. 'Parole' is the particular uses of this system, or selections from the system, which the speaker or writer makes on this or that occasion. These two aspects lead to defining stylistics, since it is the main concern of my study, as follows:
>
> Stylistics, as Leech and Short point out (1981, p. 13), can be simply defined as the study of a style which is an exercise in describing what use is made of the language.

These sentences from a student essay are almost all taken from Leech and Short's textbook *Style in Fiction* (1981). Because they are copied from it directly (with only minor changes), they make sense as individual sentences; but they do not connect together, because they come from different places in the original book. The first paragraph, for example, comes from p. 10 and the second from p. 13; and all the connections Leech and Short make between these pages have been lost, with the result that it is not clear how the first paragraph leads to the second paragraph. Moreover, because the textbook had a different purpose from the essay, it isn't clear how the material taken from the textbook is relevant to the essay's topic of foregrounding in *King Lear*. This is a general problem with copying or paraphrasing other people's work: your goals are different from theirs, and so the structure of your argument will also be different. The words of someone else's arguments are very unlikely just to fit straight into and so create a structure and argument for your own essay.

A related problem with copying other people's arguments can be seen by comparing an excerpt from a plagiarised text (a) with the essay version derived from it (b):

    (a) Stylistics, simply defined as the (linguistic) study of style, is rarely undertaken for its own sake, simply as an exercise in describing *what* use is made of language.

    (b) Stylistics, as Leech and Short point out (1981, p.13), can be simply defined as the study of a style which is an exercise in describing *what* use is made of the language.

In this case, the writer's revisions have turned the meaning of the original into its opposite: the original (a) says that stylistics is *rarely* an exercise in describing what use is made of language; but the revision (b) says that stylistics should be *defined as* an exercise in describing what use is made of language. This (almost certainly unintended) result is a consequence of the writer relying on other people to state ideas rather than trying to understand and restate them in her or his own voice. In general, if you can't restate someone else's ideas in your own words, it is likely that you do not yet understand them sufficiently to be able to make appropriate use of them.

    The writer of this extract may have felt that she or he was paraphrasing rather than plagiarising, and might point to the reference made in the extract to Leech and Short as evidence that she or he was not being dishonest. Nevertheless, the rewritten version conforms so closely to the original, with just isolated words changed, that it cannot reasonably be called a paraphrase. Either no words should have been changed and the original should have been presented as a quotation, or the original should have been rewritten as a paraphrase (in both cases, acknowledging that the *whole passage* comes from the textbook, something the extract above from 'Foregrounding in *King Lear*' doesn't do).

    Plagiarism often arises accidentally. For example, you may have copied directly from a book into your notes, then forgotten that your notes are not your own original work, and so incorporated them directly into your essay. And plagiarism is often the result of an admiration for the wording of the original – a feeling that such ideas could not be put better. But if you really feel this, it is usually appropriate to quote the original, rather than incorporate its words into your essay as though they are your own.

5.8   SUMMARY, SUGGESTIONS AND EXERCISES

Summary In this chapter, we have shown how you can overcome many of the local difficulties of putting the words and sentences of your essay together, including the special difficulties presented by the opening and closing passages. We have suggested techniques for creating continuity through the different sections of your essay, by linking together and signposting for a reader the various points you make. Signposting is important in many aspects of essay-writing: in showing your reader where you have got to, how your paragraphs connect together and which words are your own and which are quoted.

Specific suggestions

* Take special care with your first paragraph. Tell your reader what questions you are going to answer and don't make promises you can't keep (see pp. 92–4).
* Take special care with your last paragraph. Use it as a way of bringing the argument of your essay to a conclusion. Read the first paragraph again, but don't copy it into your last paragraph. Don't be grandiose, banal or over-personal, and don't normally end with a quotation from someone else (see pp. 95–7).
* Use topic sentences at the beginning (and sometimes also at the end) of paragraphs (see p. 99).
* Divide your essay into sections, but don't make the sections too small (see p. 100).
* Use cohesive markers, but don't expect them to create connections between unconnectable material (see pp. 100–4).
* Get into the habit of standing back from your essay so that you can comment on it for the benefit of your reader (see p. 104).
* Avoid using long quotations unless really necessary (see p. 106).
* Say where quotations come from and explain what they are doing in your essay (see pp. 107–8).
* Either rewrite thoroughly or quote exactly: in between, you are in danger of plagiarism (see pp. 109–10).

Exercises

(1) The following is a quotation from a book by Christopher Norris called *Deconstruction: Theory and Practice* (first published by Methuen, in London, in 1982).

> To present 'deconstruction' as if it were a method, a system or a settled body of ideas would be to falsify its nature and lay oneself open to charges of reductive misunderstanding.

Imagine that you are writing an essay, and want to refer to what Norris says about deconstruction. Write out a version of this quotation which is a

111

paraphrase, and another version which is a mixture of paraphrase and quotation. (see p. 105). Make sure that your text makes it clear where the quotation comes from (see pp. 107–8).

(2) The following passage is the beginning of an exam essay on the development of the modern novel. Drawing on our discussion of paragraph organisation in general, and opening paragraphs in particular (pp. 92–4), revise the passage in ways that present to best effect its main points. As you do so, try as far as possible to keep to the basic sense of the passage.

> The traditional novel writers like Jane Austen are essentially objective and descriptive, Jane Austen for example describes events and people in a basic narrative style, she has very little involvement with any kind of thought life; the actions made dictate the novel almost completely. Conrad's *Heart of Darkness* is the first English modernist novel, it was written at the break of the century, a time of great change and movement (for example, electricity, airplanes, telephone were all invented, democracy and freud emerged.) Writers at this time were exploring the new social and material world in which they lived. The fundamental difference between the traditional novel and this the new novel is that now the style is analytical and psychological. Novels involve thoughtlifes and motives, feelings and attitudes. T.S.Eliot for example wrote a series of poems about the disillusionment of modern life, these poems are a comment on the repition of day to day life in the city.

5.9 YOUR OWN NOTES ON THIS CHAPTER

1

2

3

4

5

CHAPTER SIX

Grammar, punctuation and spelling

You may have learned English as a child or as an adult. But no matter how fluently you speak English you are likely to have at least some problems when you write it. This chapter is about a number of the problems you may face in writing words (e.g. spelling) and in writing sentences (e.g. punctuation and 'grammar'). This chapter comes *after* the chapter on writing the essay because it is likely to be most useful to you when you come to re-read and correct what you have written.

6.1 MISTAKES AND VARIATION

Different users of English speak and write English differently. Whereas Scots generally write 'colour' and Australians write 'I know the answer', Americans generally write 'color' and Indians in many circumstances write 'I am knowing the answer'.

No one owns English, and no one has a natural right to tell other English speakers how to use it. When people publish prescriptive grammar books, or dictionaries which tell you how to spell words or style manuals which tell you how to punctuate, they are either making their own choice between different possible (in many cases, arbitrary) rules or conforming to rules which have been selected at some point by others from a range of possibilities and passed down through history. Of course, just because a rule could have been different doesn't mean that you should ignore it. If you ignore the rule which tells you to drive down the left-hand side of the road in Britain you may crash your car. Similarly, you can 'crash' your essay by breaking the most influential – though finally arbitrary, simply conventional – rules of writing.

Here is an example. Some people write 'it's cover' (as in 'the book has on it's cover'), with possessive 'it' followed by apostrophe and 's'. Books which give rules of punctuation will tell you that this is a mistake. Possessive 'its' should be written without an apostrophe, just as possessive 'his' is written without an apostrophe; only the 'it's' which means 'it is' should be written with an apostrophe.

Should you follow this rule or not? It would be possible to argue that 'it's cover' is just a different convention of punctuation, rather than a mistake. Perhaps it is not in the grammar books because the grammar books do not reflect how people actually use language. You can accordingly make a decision about using *it's* or *its* on the basis of what you gain and what you lose. Using a variation (possessive *it's*) means that you are asserting your right to your own language; but you may well also alienate your reader, who might decide that, at least in her or his view, 'you can't write properly'. The variation might help your reader understand you and your writing, or it might hinder understanding of what you write. In the end, you have to make your own decision. But it is useful to know what the conventional rules are, and also to bear in mind who you are writing for. The relationship between you and your reader(s), especially in academic courses, is not generally an equal one. So this is one further factor to consider as you weigh up the alternatives. One solution to the problem is to think of the prescribed forms of standard written English as a sort of register: a variety to be used for specific purposes (including writing coursework essays and exam answers) which nevertheless may not be a variety that you identify much with, by comparison with the usage of your family and friends.

In the rest of this chapter we discuss some common errors (or variations) in spelling, grammar and punctuation. (Note that we consider the related issues of the role of active and passive grammatical constructions in writing style elsewhere, in Chapter 4, pp. 83–4, and the use of inverted commas round quotations in Chapter 5, p. 106.)

6.2 SPELLING AND HOW WORDS ARE PUT TOGETHER

A written word is a combination of letters, while a spoken word is a combination of sounds. Letters do not correspond exactly to sounds, with the consequence that knowing how to pronounce a word doesn't necessarily mean you know how to spell it (and vice versa).

This mismatch between speaking and spelling leads to SPELLING MISTAKES. Spelling mistakes do not usually stop your writing being understood, but in many contexts they carry undesirable connotations which you may wish to avoid ('doesn't read', 'illiterate', 'badly taught', etc.). Like any rules, spelling rules can be broken for particular effect, as in the poet Ezra Pound's dismissive spelling of 'culture' as 'kulchur', or the hostile spelling of 'America' as 'Amerika'.

Some of the differences between letters and sounds are:

- the letters are the same wherever English is used, but the sounds of English (particularly vowel sounds) change dramatically from region to region;
- there are far fewer letters than sounds, so that, for example, the five written vowels have to stand for two to three times as many spoken vowels;
- two letters can stand for one sound (the letter-pair 'sh' stands for a single sound), and one letter can stand for a sequence of two sounds (in our dialect, 'o' in the word 'no' stands for two sounds in sequence, a vowel first, followed by a 'w' sound made with the lips);
- the spelling of English was more or less fixed several hundred years ago; but the pronunciation keeps changing, so that even where a letter once corresponded more or less to a sound, now it may not;
- there are (often rather obscure) conventions which have been adopted about spelling, which need to be learned. One example is the rule 'i before e except after c' (hence 'believe' not 'beleive', but 'conceive' not 'concieve').

Understanding general differences between spelling and speaking may help you to improve your own spelling, and may make it more interesting to focus on spelling as an issue in your writing. And there is another aspect of the construction of a word which it may also be helpful to know something about: that some (particularly longer) words are built out of other words, by adding prefixes at the beginning or suffixes at the end.

One simple example of this relates to the use of *'s*, discussed in the previous section. This is an example of a SUFFIX, which enables you to take a word and build another word from it. You can take the noun *John*, then add *'s* and make a new word, 'John's', meaning 'belonging to John'. (With nouns in the plural, such as *students*, the convention is simply to add an apostrophe, as in 'the students' books'; with names already ending in 's', apostrophe 's' is still generally added – so *Keats's*, rather than *Keats'*, though the apostrophe without an additional 's' is nearly always used for ancient classical names, as in *Augustus'*.) What is interesting here, however, is that the word *its* (the possessive pronoun, meaning 'belonging to it') is not built by taking *it* and adding *'s* to it. Instead (and this runs against our intuitions, hence the likelihood of mistakes in this area), *its* is a single, complete word which does not contain a suffix. So it is worth remembering that there is another, different suffix, *s*, which expresses plural and which does not have an apostrophe. You can take *poem*, add *s*, and get the plural *poems*; *poem's* is accordingly an incorrect way of writing the plural of *poem* because you have used the wrong suffix. (Use of *'s* to indicate plurals is a very common error in essays, especially with dates: so, *the 1920s*, not *the 1920's*.)

Thinking about the way a word is put together can sometimes help you to remember how to spell it. You can remember how to spell 'repetition' (not 'repitition'), for instance, by remembering the related word 'repeat' which has 'e'; 'repetition' is made by adding the suffix 'ition' to 'repeat' (and then cutting out the 'a'). Even the notorious 'one consonant or two?' problem can sometimes be solved this way: 'reccommend' can be seen to be the wrong spelling because the word is made by adding the prefix 're' to the word 'commend'. It is even possible to use this method when there is no suffix involved: you can remember how to spell 'separate' (not 'seperate') by linking it with the loosely related word 'pair'.

It is often possible, then, to understand and so overcome spelling errors, once you understand why you are making an error and can work out a way of reminding yourself of the correct form. For example, if you spell 'existence' as the incorrect 'existance', you could try to understand why – in this case, because there are two suffixes, one '-ence' and another '-ance', and you have chosen to add the wrong one to 'exist' (the two suffixes are confusingly pronounced basically the same). Spelling 'incorporate' as the incorrect 'encorporate' is similar, this time because you have chosen the prefix 'en' instead of the prefix 'in'. For each word you have problems spelling, try to think of a reason why. Even if the reason doesn't seem fully convincing, or seems in itself unimportant, the process of analysing the word can sometimes serve as a trigger which enables you to remember the correct spelling.

Thinking about why you make particular mistakes (rather than just resigning yourself to being 'a bad speller') is one way of overcoming spelling problems. It is also important to develop the habit of checking words in your own writing. Do this *as a separate routine* after writing if you are concerned not to interrupt the flow of composition. Use a dictionary – almost any English dictionary is adequate for this purpose; and check all words of which you are even a little unsure. It is easy to become complacent and just feel that most of the words are probably right even when they aren't. However you organise your checking routine, it is crucial to present written work which has been checked over for spelling. The credibility of your work will suffer severely if key words, such as technical terms or people's names, are misspelled. After all, what would you, as a reader – even as a reader sympathetic to language variation and unpersuaded by prescriptive manuals – be likely to make of an essay on symbolism which repeatedly tells you that things are 'symbollic'?

6.3 GRAMMAR: HOW SENTENCES ARE PUT TOGETHER

Grammatical errors and grammatical variations can arise when you put words together into phrases and phrases together into a sentence. There has been a lot of work – both recently and in different traditions over a very long historical period – on how sentences are put together. The details of how sentences work are very complicated; and even now no one understands fully what the actual rules governing the combination of words and phrases in any given language are. (It is possible to learn about aspects of sentence structure by studying linguistics, specifically the part of linguistics called SYNTAX.)

One by-product of investigations into grammar has been the production of introductory books like *Teach Yourself English Grammar*, and *A University Grammar of English*, which provide accounts of most basic aspects of sentence formation. What we say in this chapter is simplified. But we hope it will be helpful with some of the more common grammatical problems writers run into. Before beginning our discussion, however, we should perhaps emphasise once more the distinction between an error and a variation. Class, regional and ethnic variation is a source of difference between people as regards ways of writing a sentence; but, just as in spelling, there are STANDARD forms of written grammar, which are intended to override differences and be common to everyone. Even so, there is no unchallengeable rule book or authority you can turn to which will tell you exactly what is standard and what is not.

6.4 GRAMMATICAL WORDS AND THE USE OF 'THE'

GRAMMATICAL WORDS typically have very specialised meanings and can be particularly difficult for non-native speakers to learn. Among the grammatical words which cause problems are the prepositions (words like 'of', 'on', 'to', etc.); choosing the right one can sometimes be difficult, as in the following example:

impediments *of* industrial advances

The preposition here should be *to*. Grammatical words and grammatical objects like suffixes (as we have seen – expressing possession, plurality or past/present tense) are a particular problem in writing, particularly for non-native speakers, and we will see further examples of this.

One of the hardest problems to confront, though, is the correct use of 'the' (the definite article), a word which has no direct equivalent in many languages. Here are some sentences (written by people whose first language is not English) where we would *not* have used 'the':

> No movement in *the* **British literary history** before Aestheticism . . .
>
> Art deals with *the* **non-existent, unreal, abstract and decorative images**.
>
> I want to undertake *the* **postgraduate study in Britain**.

Now here are two cases where we think 'the' *should* have been used (__ indicates where we would put 'the'):

> In __**1950s** the Theatre of the Absurd developed.
>
> . . . and were part of the hierarchic domesticity which society, __ **bourgeoisie** in particular, acted upon.

Even though we can be quite sure that we would use 'the' in these examples, it remains difficult to explain exactly how we decide. This is typical of what it involves to speak a language fluently: you can do something consistently and in agreement with other speakers without being able to explain why. This description of 'fluency' is hardly helpful to anyone who is having difficulty with English grammar or idioms, however. So what we will try to do is to work out a preliminary understanding of the conventions which tell English speakers when to use 'the'. As elsewhere in this chapter (and book), our basic assumption is that understanding leads to learning.

'The' is used to introduce a NOUN PHRASE, or a group of words centring on a noun which together name something (the noun phrase is given in boldface in the above examples). What 'the' does is to tell the reader that what the noun phrase names is something (or belongs to a group of things) which is already familiar to the reader. In the above examples, 'the' has a meaning something like 'the phrase which follows names something which belongs to a group which is already familiar to you'. So we say 'the 1950s' because, as part of an implied group of decades (the 1940s, the 1960s, etc.) the 1950s form part of a common way of categorising the passing years. And we say 'the bourgeoisie' because the bourgeoisie forms part of a familiar group of class types: the working class, the upper class, etc. It is exactly this kind of function which gives the first three examples their odd effect. By saying 'the postgraduate study', the writer is implying that there is a familiar group of types of study – the undergraduate study, the postdoctoral study, etc., rather like the classification of decades or social classes. But this intuitive classification does not exist in an analogous way. So the only justification for saying 'the postgraduate study' would be if the writer had already named a group of types of study (so *creating* the classification), and then compared the postgraduate element with an element of undergraduate studies. Thus something of the effect of using 'the' with postgraduate study might be seen in the following (still slightly unidiomatic) example:

> Of the two phases of study which I want to pursue, I want to undertake *the* postgraduate study in Britain and the undergraduate study in America.

Our discussion of these examples suggests that you can use 'the' if you have already created a situation where you are naming a group of which the 'the' phrase indicates a subgroup. Consider in this light the following modification to one of the other examples given above; all we have done is to add a group of things ('kinds of images') of which the relevant phrase can be treated as a part:

> There are various kinds of images which can be explored. Art deals with *the* non-existent, unreal, abstract and decorative images. Science deals with the existent, real, concrete and functional images.

One problem for the non-native speaker of English is to decide when a group can be assumed to be familiar. For example, the group 'types of class' (giving '*the* bourgeoisie') seems established, but not the group 'types of study' (so disallowing '*the* postgraduate study'). Knowing these sorts of convention seems to be as much part of knowledge of the culture as knowledge of the language. So solving the difficulty involves a combination of understanding with memorisation of particular examples.

6.5   THE PRESENT AND THE PAST

TENSE, the grammatical expression of time, is a source of two distinct kinds of problem, each of which we should consider.

One problem relates to the grammatical word 'have' when it is used to express past tense (the 'perfect' use of 'have'):

Women *have* been particularly targeted in magazines, especially during the Second World War, when the British government *has* realised the importance of women's magazines as a channel of communication.

Native speakers of English typically use 'have' in the present tense (as in these two examples) only when they want to imply that the event described is still happening or is still the case. So we understand the first 'have' to mean that women are still targeted – which in this instance probably isn't the meaning the writer intends. The second 'have' (= 'has') seems odd because the realisation happened only during the Second World War and is now clearly finished.

The second problem involving tense relates to whether you should use the present or the past tense in your writing. It is generally the present tense which is used when you describe a text, even when you describe it in terms which place it in the past (e.g. by mentioning the author):

In *Los Gusanos* (1991) John Sayles describes Miami as it was in the early 1980s. He constructs a complex set of interrelationships between the different ethnic groups.

It would sound odd to put this description into the past tense, with 'described' and 'constructed', unless you were deliberately emphasising the the fact that this book was produced at a particular point in the past, for example in order to compare it explicitly with a book written more recently. The present tense is generally also used when telling a story, as in a summary of the narrative of a novel. The present tense is used in this case because it carries a sense of immediacy and impact. Past tense, on the other hand, is generally used for describing situations or narrating events *outside* the work(s) you are discussing, such as those of national or cultural history or the development of literary traditions.

Once you have decided which tense to use for a particular section of your essay, check that you are consistent – do not for example start a narrative in one tense and later change into another, unless you have a very good reason for doing so.

6.6 CO-REFERENCE

One of the techniques of cohesion (see Chapter 5, p. 100) is that instead of repeating a phrase, it is possible to use what are called grammatical words like pronouns 'it', 'he', 'she', 'they', or demonstratives like 'this'. However, this too can be a source of writing difficulties.

Usually you would use the demonstrative 'this' rather than the pronoun 'it' to refer to a text; that is, you would not do as the following writer has done:

> *Serrusalmus* by Lesley Glaister. It is about an amazing patient of 'Agoraphobia', Marjorie.

Instead, the writer should have simply combined these into a single sentence without 'It', or kept two sentences but replaced 'It' with 'This text'.

A common problem with co-referential items like pronouns and demonstratives arises when it is not clear what they refer to:

> Sir William Lucas is 'in earnest contemplation of the greatness before him' and his daughter Maria 'frightened almost out of her senses' when they meet Lady Catherine at Rosings, which expresses their simplicity and nature to be easily impressed by grandeur and presentation. This is not surprising, since Sir William had been knighted . . .

The difficulty here lies in what 'this' refers to in the second sentence. Is it (a) how Sir William Lucas feels, or (b) how Maria feels, or (c) the relation between their feelings and their 'simplicity and nature', or (d) some combination of these? (Notice, too, an analogous problem with 'which' in the preceding sentence.) The writer of this essay should have noticed the possibility of an ambiguity or difficulty for the reader in tracing the reference back, and could have solved the problem by replacing the ambiguous word 'this' with a phrase which makes clear who or what is being referred to, such as, perhaps '*That Sir William should feel this* is not surprising since he had been knighted.'

6.7   SUBJECT AND VERB

The beginning of most written sentences fits a pattern or template which we can represent like this:

> subject phrase – (optional) auxiliary verbs – verb . . .

The SUBJECT is a phrase: usually a group of words, generally centred around a noun, which together name something. Between the subject and the verb there can be various words, including the perfect 'have' discussed in the last section (an example of an optional auxiliary verb). Two familiar mistakes in written English (made even by fluent native speakers) occur between the subject and the verb: one involves 'agreement', the other involves punctuation. We look first at the agreement problem, and come to the punctuation problem as part of a more general discussion of punctuation.

In many grammar books you will find a rule which says that the subject AGREES WITH the verb. This rule refers to the fact that a subject which is (or is centred around) a singular noun is followed by a verb which has the suffix *s* added to it. In older forms of English (roughly until the sixteenth century), and in many other languages, there is much more agreement than this; so it may be the leftover, or residual nature of agreement in English which is the source of its difficulty. Certainly some dialects of English (such as Urban Black English in the USA) have developed further, to the point where there is no agreement at all.

Here are some examples where the subject does not agree with the verb (i.e. these will therefore generally be classed as 'mistakes'). The main noun in the subject is boldfaced, the verb is italicised.

> The **study** of commercial advertisements in general *aim* to isolate a single issue.
>
> **Advocates** of Northrop-Frye-style genre analysis *believes* . . .
>
> The **analysis** of the adverts *demonstrate* that . . .
>
> The **use** of ambiguity and puns *are* another feature . . .

In each of these sentences the subject contains several nouns. And in each subject, the central noun (the one in bold face which defines the basic meaning of the subject) is the first one. The writers have mistakenly made the verb agree not with this noun but with the final noun in the subject. For example, in the first case, it is the **study** which aims to isolate the issue (and so 'study' should agree with the verb), and not the **advertisements** which aim to isolate the issue.

The following sentence shows a slightly different (but also common) agreement error.

> This chapter deals with the different linguistic **choices** that *shapes* women's magazine advertisements.

Shapes should agree with **choices** (i.e. it should be '**choices** that *shape* . . .') but the intervening 'that' seems to have interfered, as though it is taken to be a singular subject.

A third common agreement error involves sentences which begin with 'There is' or 'There are', with the real subject shifted to later in the sentence. It is this shifted subject which decides whether the verb is singular 'is' or plural 'are':

In some cases there *was* plenty of **references** to the protagonist's body parts.

Here the verb should have been 'were' because of plural 'references'.

Another common error involving the match between subject and verb involves unrelated (or so-called 'dangling') participles, which occur when a participle used at the beginning of a sentence does not match with the grammatical subject of the sentence. (A PARTICIPLE is a verb form ending in '-ing' or '-ed'.) Unrelated participles do not usually seriously impede a reader's understanding, but they are generally considered incorrect forms. Consider the following example (with the unrelated participle italicised):

> *Having* discussed this poem's beginning, the next stanza shows a marked change of mood.

The writer means that she or he has discussed the poem's meaning, but the sentence literally says that the next stanza discusses the poem's beginning (an unintended meaning). This is because 'the next stanza' is interpreted as the subject of the dangling participle. Compare:

> *Encouraged* by the success of her early publications, Charlotte Brontë gave over increased amounts of time to writing.

Here, by contrast, it is Charlotte Brontë who is the implied subject of 'encouraged'; and she is also the grammatical subject of the sentence. So in this last example the participle form does match up and produces a grammatically well-formed sentence.

6.8 PUNCTUATION

Punctuation is a way of showing your reader the structure of your sentences: it separates successive units (such as sentences by full stops, or items in a list by commas) and specifies what function words have (for example when an apostrophe indicates possession). Conventions of punctuation have changed (and some writers, such as William Blake, Emily Dickinson and Samuel Beckett, have experimented with different, personalised conventions). The basic conventions for the four most common punctuation marks are:

The FULL STOP (also called a PERIOD or FULL POINT)
Put a full stop (.) at the end of a complete sentence (i.e. a sentence which at least contains a verb). Be careful not to break up a sentence with a full stop:

Although she was a mentally ill person who lived in her own mind and was allocated a limited number of mental processes. She was determined to act, to do something about this predator.

Here, the writer has put a full stop between 'processes' and 'she', probably because the whole sentence (with a comma instead of a full stop) would have been long. But this is incorrect because the 'Although . . . processes' clause is adverbial (see below under discussion of commas,), and so should be separated from the 'She . . . predator' part by a comma.

SEMICOLON
Put a semicolon (;) between two complete clauses (in linguistics often called 'sentences') to make them one larger sentence:

The next verse is significantly longer than the first; this can be understood as a symbolic representation of the importance of its contents.

Whenever you use a semicolon, note that you also had the option of using a full stop instead. Putting two sentences together into one sentence, instead of keeping them as separate sentences, indicates a certain degree of closeness between them. ('Closeness' here means association of meaning or way of dealing with related topics, not simply physical closeness.)

COLON
Put a colon (:) between two complete clauses to make them one larger sentence:

The difference between Pip and the other characters appears again when we see how people deal with this: Pip continues to show Estella that he still wants her, never giving up.

This 'instruction' for how to use a colon is the same as the instruction for how to use a semicolon. Both are used to put two sentences together into one. The specific effect of using a colon instead of a semicolon is to suggest that what comes next is a more specific example, or an explanation, of what was said in the first sentence. Thus colons are used to expand and explain; semi-colons tend to introduce thoughts connected in other ways.

COMMA
The comma (,) is the most commonly used punctuation mark inside a sentence. It is not normally used between two complete sentences (where a semicolon or colon is used instead), but is used to separate off various supplementary things in a sentence. These include:

* Two complete sentences where the second sentence begins with 'and', 'but', or 'or' (though this usage varies depending on the 'dialect' of written English you use):

  This is Dickens's final comment, and in future he avoided the topic of school education.

* A comment (not in itself a complete clause) about the main clause – like the comments in italics below, which may include indications of time, place and manner (and which are called ADVERBIALS):

  Whenever she leaves the house, the heroine seems to become bolder.

  Lawrence concentrated on writing rather than painting, *which was fortunate*.

* Additional information is added in a phrase or clause placed next to (in APPOSITION with) something already named in the sentence which it also refers to. In such cases, commas are placed *both before and after* the added phrase or clause (which is italicised in the examples which follow).

  Melville's great novel, *Moby Dick*, is in many ways a troublesome one.

  The pagan, *who with his tattoos and shrunken heads appears to be a terrible savage in the beginning*, turns out to be the most noble character in the novel.

Many writers incorrectly put a comma only before the appositive element and forget to put one after it as well. Generally, when you wish to punctuate a piece of optional, additional information or an aside that you are embedding in the middle of a sentence – for example with commas, dashes or brackets – then whatever punctuation you use should be placed both before and after the added element to signal its boundaries, not just at one end or the other.

In many cases, however, despite the existence of general conventions it remains a writer's personal decision whether to use a comma or not. Some people like using commas and others prefer not to. Commas help your reader to understand the structure of a sentence, but like any other kind of detailed structuring they risk interfering with reading instead of helping it. Punctuation has sometimes been used to imitate the pauses a speaker might make if reading a sentence aloud, and commas often keep something of this function still.

As an example of how punctuation rules work, consider the rule which forbids you inserting a comma to separate the subject and the verb.

Despite this rule, writers commonly do this, as can be seen from the following examples:

> The quasi-totality of students in my department, *opted* for English
> . . .

> However, a close analysis of his individual texts, *has been under-researched* . . .

> Existing biographical, historical and philosophical works on Oscar Wilde, *have enhanced* our knowledge and understanding of his literary personality . . .

These are interesting cases of punctuation. It is possible that the writers may have decided, in each case, that the rule had to be broken in order to help the reader follow the sentence. Evidently in each sentence the purpose of the comma is to tell you that an unusually long subject has finished and that the verb is about to follow. But is it a good idea to break the punctuation rule, even for such a reason? It is arguable that the reader may actually be confused rather than helped by the deviation from convention, precisely because she or he is expecting you to conform to the rules of punctuation. The question of keeping to convention versus innovating is particularly acute in this kind of example; and on balance it may be a good idea to reformulate problematic sentences slightly so that they can follow punctuation conventions and be clear at the same time.

Another place where writers put commas 'illegally' is between a verb which describes saying and the sentence which presents what is said:

> . . . what John Clarke *calls*, 'the subcultural bricoleurs' . . .

This example is an interesting one because different people have different views about whether or not it is in fact 'illegal'. We think the writer probably used a comma here in imitation of a similar kind of example, 'John Clarke said, "these are subcultural bricoleurs . . ." ' We ourselves would not have used a comma in the example above because we think in that example there is a greater degree of interdependence between the parts of the sentence.

In this rather similar example, however, we think it is much clearer that the comma is a mistake and far less likely that it is simply a style variant:

> This has the implication *that*, novel-writing in Wales . . .

The writer probably put a comma to indicate that a new sentence was starting. But the comma confusingly hides the close grammatical relation between 'implication that' and the sentence which follows.

Our way of viewing these difficulties with commas suggests a significant point about punctuation in general: you use commas (and other forms of punctuation including dashes and brackets round parentheses such as this one) where there are identifiable breaks between the parts of a sentence. You use semicolons and colons to indicate specific relationships between sentences that you wish to connect together into a larger, composite sentence. But decisions about exactly when to use each type of punctuation vary from writer to writer. It is difficult to establish precise rules. As you punctuate, however, remember that departures from convention result in writing which appears incorrect and which can be difficult to understand.

6.9 SUMMARY, SUGGESTIONS AND EXERCISES

Summary The main point we have made in this chapter is that in a relatively formal style such as that of academic essay-writing, much of the impact and credibility of what you write is achieved by the way it conforms to conventions. Such conventions cover many aspects of writing, including grammar, spelling and punctuation; and for this reason, it is important to develop routines to ensure that your work is presented appropriately in these areas. Working through a series of commonly occurring problems, we have identified relevant conventions and suggested strategies for avoiding mistakes.

Specific suggestions

* Where spelling is concerned, try to understand your mistakes in terms of the relationship between sounds and letters, and the construction of some words out of suffixes and prefixes. Understanding sources of error may help you to remember correct forms (see pp. 116–17).
* Check over your drafts, and separate the overall process of writing from the more mechanical process of checking for correct spellings, grammar, etc. (see p. 117).
* Use reference books, to help you understand your mistakes and to act as a guide (see p. 118).
* If you are not a native speaker of English, learn where your weak spots are and check them; you may well have problems with choosing the right preposition, inserting 'the' correctly, or using 'have' with the correct meaning (see pp. 119–21).

* Use the present tense for describing the content of a text or narrating the story. Make sure that you use tense consistently in a passage (see p. 121).
* Use a pronoun only when it is completely clear what it refers to (see p. 122).
* Pay particular attention to the relationship between the subject and the verb in a sentence: check agreement, watch for unrelated participles, and remove intervening commas as necessary (see pp. 122–4).
* Remember that a semicolon can be used instead of a full stop, but a comma normally cannot (see p. 125).
* Use commas to help your reader understand the structure of your sentences (see pp. 125–8).

Exercise

(1) The following passage, which is the closing section of an essay on the central issues raised by the play *Hamlet*, contains a number of spelling, punctuation and grammatical errors. Using suitable reference sources if necessary, correct the mistakes in the way that you might do going through a piece of your own before submission. At the same time, amend other aspects of presentation (such as register, use of quotations, etc.) in ways suggested in this and previous chapters.

> Hamlet is up against not just a man, but a king, he will have to strike when the king is unarmed, And he would also have to be able to explain his actions, and yet even his mother does not believe him, but only see him as mad
>
> 'Hamlet thou has't cleft my heart in twain.'
>
> To conclude, the play does give us the answers to the questions we demand from Hamlet, we understand the delay's he makes in killing Claudius due to the nature of his thoughts, he is concerned with the future of his soul and this seems to me the central issue in Shakespeare's *Hamlet*.

6.10 YOUR OWN NOTES ON THIS CHAPTER

1

2

3

4

5

CHAPTER SEVEN
Completing

Even when you have finished the main stages of writing, and have presented your essay in a suitable format, there are still jobs to be done. In this chapter, we consider those jobs. But first, we need to establish how you know that you have finished.

7.1 HOW DO YOU KNOW WHEN YOUR WORK IS FINISHED?

Literary studies is an open-ended discipline. Final answers and fixed conclusions are almost meaningless notions because the problems you raise – having to do with culture, emotion and meaning – are extremely complicated. This can mean that it is difficult to finish an essay in literary studies, because of the almost philosophical difficulty of knowing what finishing would mean.

Writing an essay involves trying to pull something coherent out of this complexity. So one way of considering 'completion' is to ask: have I answered the question I raised at the beginning of my essay? This is a good reason for beginning your essay by formulating a question as specifically as possible (see Chapter 1, p. 13). Only if your essay has a clear goal is it possible to decide whether that goal has been reached.

Another way of deciding on completeness is to ask whether your essay is completely understandable from beginning to end. Your argument is not complete until it can be understood, step by step, as someone reads through it.

Often, you will be writing to an external deadline and prescribed word limit, which themselves tell you when you are finished. Their arbitrariness is what makes them useful – they help you ignore the actual open-endedness of literary studies. Word and time limits force you to rank tasks in terms of relative priority; and then you have an automatic way of deciding whether lower priority tasks are achievable.

It's also worth recognising the existence of a syndrome which we might call COMPLETION ANXIETY. Sometimes your writing seems unfinished for reasons which have nothing to do with the essay or dissertation itself. You may be simply worrying that your work isn't good enough, or isn't yet ready to let other people see. To counter these worries, remember that nothing is ever as good as it could be, and that in the end you have to separate your writing from yourself. A judgement on your writing is not a judgement on you as a person; and in any case you are so familiar with your work that you will see problems that no one else will notice. This is a good reason for asking someone else to read your work; many things which appear to you to be basic problems may not trouble another reader at all.

7.2 PRODUCING A SUMMARY, TABLE OF CONTENTS, ABSTRACT AND INDEX

When you decide whether you are going to read something, it is useful first to read a summary of it. Dissertations and some essays begin with a summary, called an ABSTRACT, which has this purpose. The abstract should tell the potential reader what is in your work. In the space of less than a page you should try to describe (a) the problems you try to solve, (b) the solution you propose, and (c) name some of the texts you look at Your abstract is an advertisement for your work, to attract prospective readers; so it is important.

. If your essay or dissertation has named sections and subsections, you should add a TABLE OF CONTENTS at the beginning. The first purpose of this is to tell the reader exactly what she or he will find in your essay, and which page to find it on. There is a second purpose. Like an abstract, a table of contents should require you as its writer to look at and decide what is in your essay, to outline its development. You should be able to read your own table of contents (or abstract) and get a sense of what the essay says. If titles of sections are vague or uninformative (or boring or clichéd), it may be that these sections lack focus and purpose. If you can't see any clear development when you look at the table of contents, perhaps it is because the essay has failed to have any clear development and is not yet finished.

132

It is. useful when a published book has an INDEX, and with a long dissertation (e.g. an MA, MPhil, MLitt or PhD thesis) you will help your reader if you also provide one. Indexes have several uses. They tell your reader where to find discussion of particular topics. They also act as a guide to what your thesis contains – and to what you think is important in it because you have chosen to index it. You might index people's names (including the names of authors you cite), titles of important books, and topics. Names and titles are easy to index because they are easily identified in the text; you can even ask someone else to do this for you. But topics are harder to index. Usually you decide on which topics to index as you read through your work; but you may realise that a topic should be indexed only when you find that you have referred to it several times. So making an index generally involves more than one reading of your dissertation. There are, incidentally, books which give rules for writing indexes (such as M.D. Anderson's *Book Indexing*). We suggest, however, that you deal with each rule as you would deal with any rule for writing: use it if you are required to (for example, by an assessor), or if it genuinely helps the reader and achieves an effect you want; otherwise, ignore it.

7.3 THANKING PEOPLE, AND OTHER ACKNOWLEDGEMENTS

The ACKNOWLEDGEMENTS, at the beginning of a published work or dissertation, allow you to thank people and organisations. If you have been given permission to reproduce material, you will usually have to thank the authors or publishers who have given the permission. Often you will have had useful discussions with people, or may have used their ideas; these people's names should be included. You may want to emphasise, following convention, that you take complete responsibility for the way ideas are represented, even if they are not your own, so that any mistakes will not be blamed on the people you have named. There are also forms of institutional help which might be acknowledged, including technical help (e.g. typing) given to you, or financial help given to you by a funding body. Finally, in a research dissertation you should say if any part of your thesis or essay is related to conference papers you have given or articles you have published; one side-effect of this is to show that your work has already gained some degree of acceptance and circulation.

7.4 PUTTING TOGETHER A BIBLIOGRAPHY

In your essay or dissertation you will have referred to books and articles. You don't need to give all the details about the book (such as the first name of the author, or the publisher, or the edition) in the text itself because these details can be provided in your BIBLIOGRAPHY. (See Chapter 5, pp. 107–8 for discussion of how to cite books and articles.)

The details you write for each text in a bibliography and the order in which you list those details will depend on the rules you follow for your bibliography (e.g. the *MHRA Style Book* rules, or the *Chicago Manual of Style* rules, or rules your teacher gives you, or even just consistent rules you make up for yourself). Different books or people will give you different instructions; for example the British *MHRA Style Book* (3rd edn,1981) tells you to put just the place of publication, while the American *MLA Style Manual* (1985) has both place and publisher. Either way, it helps your reader if you are consistent in how you put your bibliography together. If you don't have access to any clear rules, or if the rules themselves are unhelpful as regards answering a particular problem, you should be guided by the principle that the purpose of bibliographical references is to enable yourself or another reader to find the work referred to, or an equivalent work.

In Chapter 2, pp. 43–4 we gave advice about the kinds of information you might store about a book or article; and most of this information will go into the bibliographical reference. Each reference usually includes both the publisher and the place of publication, partly to help identify the book further, and partly because different versions might be published by the same publisher in different places. If you find yourself in doubt, and do not have an authoritative guide you can follow (such as *MHRA* or *MLA*) to hand, then model your reference on well-established sources. We offer two sample bibliographical entries for use as models:

> Sperber, D. and D. Wilson (1986), *Relevance: Communication and Cognition*. Oxford: Basil Blackwell.
> McIntosh, A. (1963), 'As you like it': a grammatical clue to character, *Review of English Literature* 4 (2): 68–81.

A number of details should be noted in conventions for presenting bibliographical information:

* In the case of joint-authorship, give full names linked by 'and'. Only the first name should appear in reverse order (family name, initials); subsequent names should appear in the form initials followed by family name.
* Give details of the edition you are citing, if it is not the first edition

(such details, as well as the names of editors or translators if relevant, should be placed between the title (with any sub-title) and the name of the publisher). Remember that the edition you use sometimes affects what the work says (given that works are often corrected and revised between editions).

★ Be consistent in punctuation, when you separate elements in your description. You will quickly notice that the different systems use different punctuation conventions; except in very specialised work (particularly work drawing extensively on little-known historical documents), being consistent is more important than scrupulously observing a particular system.

If you use conventions based on the Harvard System, most books you refer to will be cited twice, once as a reference in the main body of the text, where you provide the given name (or surname) of the author and date of publication, and once with full details in the bibliography. Make sure that the citation agrees between the two places. The most common mismatch involves date of publication, and for this there are two guidelines to follow:

★ If an author has two books with the same publication date, you should distinguish them in both the text and the bibliography, using 'a', 'b', 'c', etc. after the date (see above, Chapter 5, p. 107).

★ The date given in the textual citation should be the same as the date in brackets following the author's name in the bibliographical reference; this is the date of publication of the edition you are citing. As an example of the kind of mistakes which are possible, one writer had a bibliographical listing 'Lacan, J. (1966), *Ecrits: A Selection*, English Translation 1977, Tavistock: London', but then referred to the work in the body of the text as '(Lacan, 1977)'. The reference in the text to '(Lacan, 1977)' is correct, but the dates of the editions should have been presented in the bibliography as, 'Lacan, J. 1966 (1977)', with appropriate further details of the translation later in the entry.

Sometimes a bibliography includes *more* than the articles or books you have referred to. This is common in textbooks, where further recommended reading is often added. It is unlikely that your essay or dissertation will need to make recommendations in this way, so you should include only those books which you refer to in your argument. If you want to include a book to show that you have read it (but don't actually refer to it), add a note at a relevant point which says something like 'for further discussion, see . . .' This is a legitimate way of displaying relevant reading.

A bibliography can be a single list, or you can organise it into sub-lists. A thesis on 'Ezra Pound as a Modernist Poet', for example, might have sub-lists in the bibliography entitled 'Books by Ezra Pound', 'Books on Ezra Pound', 'Books on Modernist poetry', etc. Sub-lists are useful as guides to further reading; but because there are several lists instead of one, it's less easy for the reader to match up citations in the essay with bibliographical details; you need to decide on priority between ease of reference to particular works and convenience of suitably named sub-lists.

7.5 ADDING SUPPLEMENTARY MATERIAL: FOOTNOTES AND APPENDICES

With the 'author–date' reference system, the need for footnotes to document a specific quotation or reference is minimised. In such a system, footnotes are generally restricted to one of the following purposes:

- Providing incidental comment or explanation. Don't use too many notes of this kind; though they may contribute to the 'scholarly' register, they can clog up the text.
- Providing cross-references to other parts of your own essay (as in 'See below, p. 122').
- Making acknowledgements ('I am grateful for this comment to J. Smith, personal communication').

Because many readers do not read footnotes, it is unwise to put anything into a footnote which is important in understanding the argument of the essay. In 'A' level and undergraduate essays, you are unlikely to need to use footnotes very much; indeed, you may not need to use them at all. This does not mean that your writing is insubstantial or in some way 'sub-academic'. Over-use of footnotes can be as damaging as under-use of them.

7.6 CHECKING WHAT YOU HAVE WRITTEN

Here is a list of features of your work you should check once you have finished writing and have added your abstract, bibliography, etc.

- ⋆ Check spelling. People's names are particularly likely to be mis-spelled. If your text is on a computer you might use a spell-checker to help you, though there are two kinds of problem with this: many technical terms and people's names will not be in your computer's dictionary; and the spell-checker will not notice when you have used the *wrong* word (e.g. 'were' instead of 'where').

* Check grammatical errors, such as lack of agreement between subject and verb (see p. 123).

* Now that you know what the page numbers are, add them to your table of contents.

* Check that all relevant information is in your bibliography (i.e. that some entries are not incomplete). Check that every book or article you refer to in the text is in the bibliography.

* Check that all the pages are there in all the copies, and that they are numbered continuously and are in the right order.

* Make sure you have complied with the regulations for submission (this is best done before you even start, but better late than never); the regulations may include requirements about whether the essay must be typed, whether the paper has to be a particular size or kind, what margins you should leave, etc.

7.7 MAKING SURE THAT YOU MEET YOUR DEADLINE

Towards the end of a project, you may be tired and in a hurry. What tends to go wrong at this stage are aspects of the physical production of the manuscript. If someone else is typing your essay or thesis for you, they may be away or sick at the crucial moment; so try to arrange in advance for a back-up. If you are typing your own thesis, or are printing it out on a computer printer, make sure that you have enough dark ribbons and paper, and that you are sure of access to the machine when you will need it.

Find out in advance where alternative equipment is, in case machines, such as photocopiers, break down. If you are using a computer it is particularly important to have at least one identical copy of your computer files. This means that if you accidentally destroy or misplace a file (or the disc it is on) you have an instant replacement. Even making the copies should be done as far in advance as possible.

·7.8 A VIVA VOCE EXAMINATION

'Viva voce' means 'by or with the living voice', and is the name for an oral examination (often just called a 'viva'). Sometimes (e.g. in cases of borderline marks in degree classification, or more commonly with research degrees) you have to undertake a viva examination to supplement your writing. From an institutional point of view, the purposes of a viva examination differ from culture to culture. One purpose is to check your relationship with the dissertation: that you wrote it yourself, and that you have done the reading you claim to have done. Another purpose is that of testing your understanding of your reading and your general knowledge of the field. Your viva may also explore your skills in argumentation, and offers you an opportunity to show that a borderline dissertation should be a pass. But you should also have your own agenda in a viva, viewing it as a chance to discuss, perhaps with people who may be able to offer advice and practical help for the future, a piece of work you will probably have undertaken largely in isolation.

In order to prepare for a viva you should *read* your dissertation. Identify weak spots, especially vague passages and poor arguments. You may also need to justify any attacks you make on critics or theories, so you should identify your attacks in advance and decide what to say about them. Imagine counter-arguments to what you have said, and work out ways of arguing against them. Practise summarising the argument of the dissertation for a non-specialist (your examiners may not all be specialists in the area of the dissertation); and think of implications of your work, including further questions, parallel cases or practical applications which you do not discuss but which are implied in your findings. Finally, remember that many dissertations are not accepted immediately because they have too many typographical errors in them; before the viva try to find all errors and prepare replacement pages in order to speed up the process of re-submission and final acceptance.

7.9 GETTING YOUR WORK READ MORE WIDELY

If you have put a lot of work into your essay or dissertation and you think it is genuinely of interest, you should try to make it possible for other people to get access to it. You could try to publish it, present it as a paper at a conference, or distribute it yourself. Publishing is easier when you have personal contact with a publisher or an editor. So if a journal editor or reviewer has seen you give a paper at a conference, they are more likely to look favourably on your work. Going to conferences is also a good way to make yourself known. Your viva itself is an important opportunity to make a valuable contact: your external examiner. If your viva is successful, ask the external examiner if she or he has any suggestions about where you could publish or might circulate all or part of your work.

It is important to adopt a realistic strategy from the start, however. You are more likely to succeed in reading a paper based on your work at a conference devoted to your particular area of interest, or to be able to publish an article in a journal specialising in your field, than to leap straight into a publisher's contract for a book. Get to know the current journals in your field and what conferences are being planned. You should also try to find out as much as possible about the most suitable or likely publishers of your work. Ask around and look through publishers' catalogues. The books which you have consulted should themselves provide an idea of the kind of thing publishers are interested in (though you should check the dates of the works you are looking at as possible models, since there are changing patterns and fashions in academic publishing, too). University Presses (e.g. Oxford, Cambridge, Manchester) may well be the first places to try, since they are more directly concerned with the publication of research findings and monographs or for further ideas, consult *The Writers' and Artists' Yearbook*.

Even if you do not plan to publish your essay or dissertation, it is worth photocopying it (reduced, if necessary) and sending copies to people who might be interested. If your work is fairly long (e.g. over 10,000 words), there's no need to photocopy all of it initially; it may be best first of all to send just a brief summary, in the form of an abstract and table of contents (see above, p. 132). By sending a shorter piece, you may well get a quicker reply, and can then send more only to people who are interested or willing to read what you have produced. The chances are that many (or even most) of the people you send your work to will ignore it. But some may be interested enough to maintain correspondence with you, and may be able to suggest publication possibilities. In any case, feedback will establish that the effort you have put into writing has not only produced the gradual (and probably unrecognised) benefits of developing your intellectual and argumentative skills, and increasing your confidence; it also contributes, if only in a small way, to wider debate concerning the topics you were interested enough in to choose to write about.

7.10 SUMMARY, SUGGESTIONS AND EXERCISES

General Summary In this chapter, we have suggested that your work is not over when you write the last word. Deciding on many aspects of presentation remains to be done, and in some cases a viva or oral defence of your work must be prepared for. Your essay can still gain further impact, by the presentation, in a suitable form, of your notes, bibliography, etc., even after you have finished writing it. When everything is complete, we suggest that you should actively seek a wider readership for your work than simply the tutor or examiner for whom it may have been written; and we offer suggestions as to how this might be achieved.

Specific suggestions

* Recognise the possibility of completion anxiety and prepare yourself to let go of your work at the appropriate time (see p. 132).
* Ask yourself whether you have actually answered the basic question which defines your essay or dissertation (see p. 132).
* Use an abstract, table of contents and index as ways of confirming the coherence of your work (see pp. 132–3).
* Use a consistent system for making references in the text and presenting bibliographical information (see pp. 134–6).
* Anticipate what might go wrong in the last few days before submission and prepare accordingly (see p. 137).
* If you are finishing a postgraduate degree, build contacts with other people; draw attention to and make arrangements to circulate your work (see pp. 138–9)

Exercises

(1) Write an abstract for a short essay which you have already written. The abstract should be no longer than two hundred words.

(2) Each of the following entries for a bibliography at the end of an essay lacks at least one item of necessary information. Although you will of course not know the relevant names or dates, etc., you *will* know what piece of information is missing. As you mark where further information is required, and of what sort, also edit the entries into an appropriate and consistent format, using the guidelines we have provided above (pp. 134–5).

Hynes S. *'Moral Models'* (1976), in Page's William Golding: Novels 1954–67.

Kinkead-Weekes M. and Gregor *William Golding, A Critical Study.* Faber and Faber, (1967).

Page N. (ed.) *William Golding: Novels* (in the Casebook Series). macmillan education Ltd. (1985).

Peter J. *The Fables of William Golding* (1957), in Page's William Golding: Novels, 1954–67
Tiger V. *William Golding, the Dark Fields of Discovery.* (1974).

7.11   YOUR OWN NOTES ON THIS CHAPTER

1

2

3

4

5

Booklist

(1) FURTHER READING ABOUT ACADEMIC WRITING AND STUDY AND RESEARCH SKILLS

Barnet, S. (1985), *A Short Guide to Writing about Literature*. Batsford

Dunleavie, P. (1986), *Studying for a Degree in the Humanities and Social Sciences*. Macmillan

Ellis, R. and K. Hopkins (1985), *How to Succeed in Written Work and Study*. Collins

Fensch, T. (1989), *Writing Solutions: Beginnings, Middles and Endings*. Hillsdale, New Jersey: Lawrence Erlbaum.

Harrison, N. (1985), *Writing English: a User's Manual*. Croom Helm

Miller, S. (1975), *Experimental Design and Statistics*. Methuen

Pirie, D. (1985), *How to Write Critical Essays*. Methuen

The Writers' and Artists' Yearbook. A. and C. Black

Watson, G. (1987), *Writing a Thesis: a Guide to Long Essays and Dissertations*. Longman

(2) BOOKS ON DEVELOPING INTERPRETATIVE AND READING SKILLS

Durant, A. and N. Fabb (1990), *Literary Studies in Action*. Routledge

Leech, G. (1969), *A Linguistic Guide to English Poetry*. Longman

Leech, G. and M. H. Short (1981), *Style in Fiction*. Longman

Lodge, D. (1992), *The Art of Fiction*. Penguin

Montgomery, M, A. Durant, N. Fabb, S. Mills and T. Furniss (1992), *Ways of Reading: Advanced Reading Skills for Students of Literature*. Routledge

(3) BOOKS ON ENGLISH LANGUAGE AND LINGUISTICS

Aitchison, J. (1972), *Teach Yourself Linguistics*. Hodder and Stoughton
Crystal, D. (1984), *Who Cares About English Usage*. Penguin
Crystal, D. (1987), *The Cambridge Encyclopedia of Language*. Cambridge University Press
Halliday, M.A.K. and R. Hasan (1977), *Cohesion in English*. Longman
Phythian, B.A. (1980), *Teach Yourself English Grammar*. Hodder and Stoughton
Quirk, R. and S. Greenbaum (1973), *A University Grammar of English*. Longman

(4) BOOKS WHICH ARE GENERALLY USEFUL IN LITERARY STUDIES

Abrams, M.H. (1981), *A Glossary of Literary Terms*, 4th edn. New York: Holt, Rinehart and Winston
Brewer, E.C. (1978), *The Dictionary of Phrase and Fable*. New York: Avenel Books
Butler, C. (1985), *Statistics in Linguistics*. Basil Blackwell
Williams, R. (1976), *Keywords: a Vocabulary of Culture and Society*. Collins/Fontana

(5) STYLE GUIDES

Atchert, W.S. and J. Gibaldi (1985), *The MLA Style Manual*. New York: The Modern Language Association of America
Maney, A.S. and R.L. Smallwood (1981), *MHRA Style book: Notes for authors, editors and writers of dissertations*, 3rd edn. Modern Humanities Research Association
(1982), *The Chicago Manual of Style: for Authors, Editors and Copywriters* 13th edn. Chicago: University of Chicago Press
Miller, C. and K. Swift (1981), *The Handbook of Non-Sexist Writing for Writers, Editors and Speakers*. Women's Press
(1981), *The Oxford Dictionary for Writers and Editors*. Oxford University Press

Index